The Software
Audit Guide

Also available from ASQ Quality Press:

The Certified Software Quality Engineer Handbook
Linda Westfall

Fundamental Concepts for the Software Quality Engineer, Volume 2
Sue Carroll and Taz Daughtrey, editors

Safe and Sound Software: Creating an Efficient and Effective Quality System for Software Medical Device Organizations
Thomas H. Faris

ISO 9001:2000: Achieving Compliance and Continuous Improvement in Software Development Companies
Vivek (Vic) Nanda

The ASQ Auditing Handbook, Third Edition
J.P. Russell, editing director

The Internal Auditing Pocket Guide: Preparing, Performing, Reporting and Follow-up, Second Edition
J.P. Russell

Quality Audits for Improved Performance, Third Edition
Dennis R. Arter

Root Cause Analysis: Simplified Tools and Techniques, Second Edition
Bjørn Andersen and Tom Fagerhaug

The Certified Manager of Quality/Organizational Excellence Handbook: Third Edition
Russell T. Westcott, editor

Six Sigma for the New Millennium: A CSSBB Guidebook, Second Edition
Kim H. Pries

Process Improvement Using Six Sigma: A DMAIC Guide
Rama Shankar

To request a complimentary catalog of ASQ Quality Press publications, call 800-248-1946, or visit our Web site at http://www.asq.org/quality-press.

The Software
Audit Guide

John W. Helgeson

ASQ Quality Press
Milwaukee, Wisconsin

American Society for Quality, Quality Press, Milwaukee 53203
© 2010 American Society for Quality
All rights reserved. Published 2009
Printed in the United States of America
13 12 11 10 09   5 4 3 2 1

Library of Congress Cataloging-in-Publication Data
Helgeson, John W.
   The software audit guide / John W. Helgeson.
      p. cm.
   Includes bibliographical references and index.
   ISBN 978-0-87389-773-0 (hardcover : alk. paper)
   1. Computer software—Validation.   2. Computer software—Verification.   I. Title.
   QA76.76.V47H45 2009
   005.1′4—dc22

                                        2009023947

ISBN-13: 978–0–87389–773–0

Publisher: William A. Tony
Acquisitions Editor: Matt Meinholz
Project Editor: Paul O'Mara
Production Administrator: Randall Benson

ASQ Mission: The American Society for Quality advances individual, organizational, and community
excellence worldwide through learning, quality improvement, and knowledge exchange.

Attention Bookstores, Wholesalers, Schools, and Corporations: ASQ Quality Press books, videotapes,
audiotapes, and software are available at quantity discounts with bulk purchases for business, educational,
or instructional use. For information, please contact ASQ Quality Press at 800–248–1946, or write to ASQ
Quality Press, P.O. Box 3005, Milwaukee, WI 53201–3005.

To place orders or to request a free copy of the ASQ Quality Press Publications Catalog, including
ASQ membership information, call 800–248–1946. Visit our Web site at www.asq.org or
http://www.asq.org/quality-press

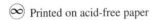 Printed on acid-free paper

Quality Press
600 N. Plankinton Avenue
Milwaukee, Wisconsin 53203
Call toll free 800-248-1946
Fax 414-272-1734
www.asq.org
http://www.asq.org/quality-press
http://standardsgroup.asq.org
E-mail: authors@asq.org

To my wonderful wife, Jeanne, for her love and patience.

Contents

Figures

Preface

The purpose of software quality audits is to monitor software development, the development process, and to help management obtain an independent view of the software development status. The purpose of this book is to improve the quality of software development audits.

Over the last 30 years I have worked in software development and software quality. I have seen people understate and mislead about the software that is being developed. I have seen poor designs, poor planning, budget overruns, missed deliveries, setbacks, mishandling, and lost data. I have seen management left in the dark on too many occasions. None of these things was planned when the project started out. It just happened along the development way. When the schedule starts to tighten, corners get cut, functions are dropped, and problems arise. Management hears about the problem when the programming team has run out of time and options. People who are backed into a corner will do crazy things.

To make effective decisions, management must have a good independent status of the specific software development. If management is made aware of problems as soon as possible, mitigation plans can be instituted in a timely manner. The software quality auditor provides the independent eyes that management needs for looking over development's shoulder and reviewing milestones. The information gleaned from software audits and reviews helps management know the answers to these questions:

- Is the project on schedule?

- What is missing or not done?

- Where are the weak areas?

- Are there any best practices?

Auditing books cover all of the basics. If you find a software section, you usually get a few paragraphs or maybe a few pages. The pages will cover configuration control and make statements about the quality of the software. Likewise, I have read software quality books that have a few paragraphs or pages about auditing. These software quality books provide only a condensed version of auditing mechanics, skimming over audit program objectives and audit administration; some may include auditor responsibilities.

For both types of books, the software audit was outside the book's main focus. They recognize the need for some sort of software audit and suggest that one should go forth and audit without giving any direction. However, the following are samples of unanswered questions:

- How do you audit software?

- What areas do you look at?

- What questions should you ask?

The answers to these questions can differ from project to project. No two projects are exactly the same. Even projects in the same company can differ or be at different points in their life cycle.

Software is not produced on a production line. The only thing that is the same on all software projects is that there is input and output. Everything in the middle is customized for the project at hand. Thus, this book does not contain a one-size-fits-all approach. It gives a choice of areas to audit and different questions that should be asked within various areas. The questions in this book are only the starting point for developing more questions for your audit. The questions have to be customized to the specific project within your organization.

I once worked for a company that performed internal software quality audits by the numbers. I don't believe that this helped the company. Looking at numbers or checking off checklists for process control is insufficient. In the 1990s process control became the big change in software development and it delivered a huge step forward in quality. Now process control has been so refined that it is getting in the way of great development. Not all software fits in one set of check boxes, and checking boxes for compliance may have little to do with real software quality.

Others have also come to the conclusion that just checking off boxes is insufficient. *Juran's Quality Handbook,* which is on most quality people's desks, states: "There is a preoccupation with blindly enforcing standards without an understanding of their usefulness."[1] David K. Watson, in the January 2006 *Quality Progress* article "Reflections on the Future of Quality," states: "Unfortunately, many companies conduct internal audits merely to ensure compliance to a standard. Little, if any real value is therefore obtained from an activity that should provide top management with critical insight and value recommendations for

---

[1] Juran and Godfrey, ed., *Juran's Quality Handbook,* 5th ed. (New York: McGraw Hill, 1999), 20.13.

improvement."[2] In addition, an article in the June 2006 issue of *Quality Digest* states, "Instead of good traffic cops—i.e., those who read procedures and catch people doing something wrong—what is needed are individuals who will be able to look at processes from a systematic viewpoint and generate ideas for improving customer satisfaction."[3] It is not auditing for the sake of auditing or compliance with a set standard; it's a tool that should be incorporated into the development process to ensure that the project is maintaining the highest level of quality.

There is a place for strict process control. When a company's process is out of control, there is a need to write procedures that will bring the process back in line. Then, the procedures should be strictly enforced until they are used routinely. Adjustments can be made to improve the procedures—refining will produce a better outcome. After process control is achieved, you will need to continue to monitor the process, but the emphasis becomes quality at the deeper level—below the procedures. There is more information about this in section 1.2, "Process and Quality."

At different times during the development life cycle, there are different focal points. At each stage of development, priorities shift and different areas become more important. Can you use the same audit at each stage? In some areas you can and in others you can't. Two different projects at the same stage might need different audit questions. I have included more than 1300 questions that an auditor could ask during an audit. The questions cover different areas at different life-cycle phases. An auditor with a background in software will have an advantage when working with my questions. However, this is not an exclusive book—rather, it is an opportunity for anyone with the mission to improve software quality through auditing. In that regard, I have explained the questions or given the reader some insight into the different areas. With this information, the auditor can expand on the questions when needed.

On the other hand, if you think that you can take only the 1300 sample questions and perform audits, please put the book down and refrain from performing audits. These questions are only a starting point, a guide (check the title of this book) to remind the auditor to look in all the corners of software development. The questions are for reference, and the auditor should create specific questions or utilize my questions for each area that is applicable. The point is to be flexible and thorough.

Here's a "heads up" for you: When procedures or processes are unchanged but development changes, the company is not moving forward. When development changes, the processes or procedures need to be reevaluated. The strict "process people" may say that procedures can be changed anytime, but they need to look

---

[2] David K. Watson, "Reflections on the Future of Quality," *Quality Progress,* January 2006, 28.
[3] Smith, Munro, and Bowen, "Internal Auditing for ISO/TS 16949," *Quality Digest,* vol. 26, no. 6 (June 2006), 35.

beyond the procedures to determine where changes are needed. Taking off the blinders and looking in all directions keeps a company up to date and allows it to move ahead of the competition. This is not revolutionary ("something totally different from what has been") but evolutionary ("a refinement of what has been").[4]

This book is divided into four sections:

Section I, Audit Fundamentals, Chapters 1–2

Section II, Audit Activities, Chapters 3–7

Section III, Audit Constants, Chapters 8–13

Section IV, Audit Functions, Chapters 14–21

I have written about two new areas that I have never seen mentioned in audit and software books (audit section): schedules as a development window and hidden software. The schedule provides a window (a view) into what is going on in development at a specific time. Knowing which tasks are behind or ahead of schedule gives the auditor new directions to pursue. Hidden software impacts the project. It may be overlooked during software development and testing, and it may be under different standards or controls than the main software. The auditor needs to be on the lookout for this hidden software and see that it is appropriately controlled. When problems with hidden software surface in the final days of a project, there will be major delays.

I wrote each chapter to be a stand-alone section of an audit. I kept the overlapping to a minimum, though you will see duplications because certain questions have more than one application. If an auditor is asked to audit a part of a system, he should be able to go directly to that chapter and use it as a reference.

My goal in writing this book is to present a broad approach that stimulates creative thinking and that ultimately results in (1) the best possible audit of software development, and (2) closing the gap between management's knowledge of the software development and the actual status of the software development. A good auditor will bridge that gap.

It is my hope that this book will open some dialogue about auditing software. Whether you agree or disagree with my views, at least give them some thought. The objective is to improve software auditing.

John W. Helgeson
ASQ CQMgr, CSQE, CQA, CQIA
authors@asq.org

---

[4]John C. Maxwell, *Developing the Leader Within You* (Nashville, TN: Thomas Nelson Publishers, 1993), 61.

Acknowledgments

John Donne in Meditation XVII said, "No man is an island, entire of itself. . ." He was speaking about the way all people are connected to one another. I am acutely aware that without the encouragement, support, and input of several people, *The Software Audit Guide* would not have been written. I owe them my thanks for their part—large or small.

First, to the ASQ Quality Press staff, Matt and Paul, and especially to Angela at Thistle Hill Publishing Services: thank you for believing that I had a valuable message. Your flexibility with deadlines, with putting my work into the hands of your esteemed review panel (including Donna Gregory, who I quoted in the book for her incisive differentiation between *verification* and *validation*), and in editing the book, were invaluable.

To the many authors I've read and whose work I cited: you are in a class by yourselves—your work inspired me and stirred my passion for software quality and auditing. Thank you Robert O. Lewis, Mark D. Baker, Daniel Galin, John W. Horch, Charles A. Cianfrani, Joseph J. Tsiakals, John E. West, B.W. Boehm, John C. Maxwell, Joseph M. Juran and A. Blanton Godfrey, David K. Watson, David Elfanbaum, Mary Beth Chrissis, Mike Konrad, Sandy Shrum, Len Fertuck, Michael Gibson, Cary Hughes, Dr. W. Edwards Deming, Nick Van Weerdenburg, Andrew S. Tanenbaum, and Maurice Halstead.

Finally, to my family. My wife, Jeanne Zacharias Helgeson: I have loved you forever. You have always believed in me and helped me to achieve my goals. You made my book a focus in our home and dedicated many long hours to discussion, editing, spelling—whatever I needed. I am so grateful for you and our life together.

Our daughter, Jan Helgeson Gardlund: you and your children make me want to be the best me I can be—your Dad, and Karli and Connor's Pop-Pop. Thank you for your typing, computer skills, and being there when you were needed. Thank you to Erik for babysitting so Jan could be available.

To Teddi M. Helgeson: your tail wags, kisses, and devotion were great stress-busters and I promise that Mom and I will be taking you back out to the park now that the book is done.

And Chris…. Believe in the impossible—follow your dreams—pigs do fly.

Part I

Audit Fundamentals

1

Introduction

This is a practical guide to auditing software. *The Software Audit Guide* will give you the questions to ask when preparing an audit. You'll find background on the questions and theoretical standards. The main objective is to do an audit and report the problems you find, while closing the gap between development and management.

It is Monday morning and you receive a call from your manager. He wants you to find out what happened in the software development department. The developers have missed a delivery for an important customer. The managers want to know "Why did we miss the delivery?" and "What is going on?" What they need but don't know to ask for is an independent audit. They want results and this book with help you perform the audit that will reveal where processes, procedures, and practices failed.

Let's look at "Why did we miss the delivery?," which is a very simple question. What does this really mean? Questions are raised right away. Whatever the reason, *it did not happen the day of delivery.* What was the reason given to management or the customer about the delivery? Why not sooner? Tracing back to the root cause, in both the delivery and communication failures, should be the main objective. Audits performed routinely at planned intervals would have highlighted weak or troublesome areas—and you wouldn't be reaching for aspirin on Monday morning.

"For want of a naile the shoe is lost, for want of a shoe the horse is lost, for want of a horse the rider is lost"

Believed to be written by George Herbert in 1651, this is a simple illustration of the need for sequencing and logic.[1]

---

[1]*Jacula Prudentum* by George Herbert was a collection of proverbs based on folklore—meaning this may not have been originally his. This information was found in an article by Stephen Frug "For Want of a Nail": from proverb to nursery rhyme June 26, 2006, available at www.gather.com/viewArticle.jsp?articleId=281474976762779

In software development all the *nails* need to be checked. That is the purpose of an audit.

A software audit is not a simple task. Management is looking for a snapshot at this moment of software development. It is time consuming and labor intensive, but worth it if you keep in mind the larger picture. Each project is different and has it own special components. There are quality principles that a project can be audited against. This is what I will do in this book: I'll show you the mechanics of what should be done to increase the chances of a successful project. Even having the mechanics right doesn't guarantee a perfect system, but it improves the odds.

In some companies software is a black hole where money is poured in and a product (or part of a product) flows out. "Find out what is going on down in that software department" and "Will they meet their schedule?" are universal management queries. Their tone denotes the level of management's frustration.

Some people think software is a magical, mystical thing. Software people (developers, designers, analysts) are often perceived as being in their own world. This is not a bad thing. It just means that outsiders do not understand their work. Time is always at a premium because coming in "under budget" is highly prized. However, cutting the development time sometimes backfires and increases the company's bottom line. It is not unusual for a development plan to be shortened because the client (meaning upper management, customer, or stakeholder) believes there is fat built into the schedule. Sometimes shortening a schedule raises the cost or the failure rate. So now there is a tight schedule to develop software and no time to write procedures or follow all the steps needed to produce a great product. In most organizations, there is a general flow for developing software; it's not written down because "everyone knows how it's done." Other times the procedures are written but the auditor needs them written in layman's English with practical not theoretical language.

How do you audit software development when you've been told that there are no written procedures and processes? Where do you start? "All roads may lead to Rome", but in software auditing a good place to begin is the Software Development Life Cycle (SDLC), which includes the processes and procedures you will need to report. (More in Chapter 2)

Some companies see software as the biggest risk factor in projects and products. Included in this factor are skill sets, schedule restraints, dependencies, new technology, and other unknowns. The rising cost of software development, with the high percentage of failures, major rewrites, slipped schedules, and cost overruns, moves right to the bottom line on companies' financial statements. Your customer deserves and expects a progress report. They are not looking for the palliative answer "Everything is fine." They are spending real money and have real expectations—they need to answer to their management, too. Sometimes the best audit; the most objective audit, is one from outside. Internal audits may be tied to personal careers, a desire to placate a difficult boss, or the need to save a project.

Nowadays management is looking outside the software development arena for independent evaluations. A project audited by an outsider, who has seen many approaches to development, might spot warning signs and encourage a project team to take corrective action. They have motion not emotion.

A programmer friend told me that all meetings with anyone higher than his direct manager were called the "rosy" meetings. Everyone knew to never bring up a problem or schedule slip, and the stock answer was "Everything is fine."

The following pie chart from the Standish report (a software industry standard) illustrates the outcome of most projects. With roughly 1/3 of all projects succeeding, there is room for improvement.

Figure 1.1 shows three categories:

- Succeeded—The project is completed on time and on budget, with all features and functions as specified.

- Challenged—The project is completed and operational, but it is overbudget and late, and it has fewer features and functions than were initially specified.

- Failed—The project is canceled before completion, never implemented, or scrapped following installation.[2]

Figure 1.1 shows that 66 percent of projects are not completed or have some other problems.

In an article in *Quality Digest,* David Elfanbaum states, "Recent studies report that less than one in three projects meet requirements, are completed on time and within budget.[3]" None of these percentages is good enough for any business.

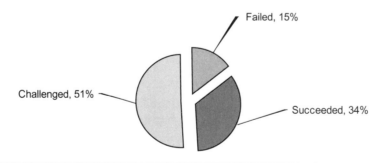

Failed, 15%

Challenged, 51%

Succeeded, 34%

Figure 1.1 2003—Standish Report.

[2]Standish Group CHAOS Report, "Latest Standish Group CHOAS Report Shows Project Success Rates Have Improved by 50%." Available from www.allbusiness.com/technology/software-services-applications-information/5739196-1.html. Accessed July 11, 2008.
[3]David Elfanbaum, "Process Improvement and Other Fairy Tales," *Quality Digest* (November 2006), 35.

With auditing we are raising the probability of success. Every department has the one employee who can give you the history of every project. What happens if he or she leaves or retires? Since auditing requires and generates documentation, the project will continue on with minimal loss of momentum.

The auditor needs a better understanding of a very complex development process. He needs to know where to ask the additional questions that pop up during the interviews. Of great importance is understanding the documents and where they fit into the system.

The employees facing the auditor sometimes feel they need to give the "right answer," which should not to be confused with an honest accounting or recitation of facts. The savvy experienced auditor will be able to differentiate fact from fiction if documentation is provided.

I am not writing this book for one application. The intent is give you a general feel for every company. If there are 10,000 software development companies or companies with software departments, there are probably 10,000 ways to develop software. I don't remember any two doing it the same way. Some functional areas have been the same, but never the whole process.

In this book, a generic procedure will be followed. It will describe the documents because it is not uncommon for the same document to go by a different name in another organization. This will enable the auditor to know where in the process the document is used.

The higher the quality of the audit, the higher the company's quality after the corrective actions have been completed.

When I hear "We have done it this way forever and we are not changing," I know they are in trouble—even if they aren't willing to face it yet. The world is changing, business models are changing. To dig in your heels and insist on doing what you're always done, will only get you what you've always gotten. In this day and market, you will probably be left in the dust and out of the competition.

A friend called to tell me that one of his internal auditors told him that he had some important fixes for his software development plan, a document that is updated yearly (company directive). He told the auditor to give him the notes or a quick write-up because they were in the last days of review for the year. The auditor told him that it would take a week or so to complete the write-up. My friend said that by contract the document needed to be finished by the end of the month. The fixes will now have to wait until next year to go in the document. My friend did not want the auditor to change his findings or not report them to management.

He wanted to do the best he could for his project and company. If you were the auditor, what would you do? The correct answer is give the notes to the manager to update the document and still have him write up the findings. It is a win-win solution. But in this case, the auditor did not and the document was updated a year later.

Audits are part of a company's quality plan; the auditor is also by default a quality person. I believe that the auditor should always put quality first. If the auditee needs information about a major finding, the auditor should explain why it needs to be fixed immediately. This is when the auditor becomes a quality mentor.

1.1 DEFINITIONS

These are words I use that might mean different things to different people:

Auditee—The company, department, or project being audited.

Auditor—An independent person who has no direct gain or loss from the outcome of the audit.

Client—The entity that authorizes the audit and pays the bill. This could be the customer or upper management.

Metric—Any measurable characteristic.

Project—Could be one program or the whole software system.

Software—Includes firmware, microcode, and documentation.

Risk—The software that is not within the customer's requirements or specifications.

1.2 PROCESS AND QUALITY

Process and quality are different functions. Process is a term to describe the list of steps to perform a task. Quality, in this usage, refers to what happens after the procedure is complete. By looking at the procedure or process used to track software problems/incidents, you will see the difference. This afternoon, I ran into someone in the parking lot. I tried to explain a quality issue in detail, and he tried to explain where it was in the process. It was as if I explained how to set up furniture in a living room, and he said you need a living room.

A company that has no quality, has to start by implementing a process. You need to fix things from the top down; clean up the gross problems. After a company has all the processes in place, the quality of the company increases by leaps and bounds.

There are places in the company for both process and quality. There are gross problems in some areas where processes are in place, and what they still need is the fine tuning of quality. You can play an untuned violin but the sound isn't as sweet. As the auditor, you must be aware of both process and quality and where they fit in each project or company. Following through once problems are detected requires commitment in tracking to completion. Dig deep—search out the root cause. Does the designer need more training? Was the designer given all the specifications? Did the design have robust features? Were the designs properly peer reviewed or, rather, rubber stamped? When the process is correct and working, then quality has been achieved.

1.3 QUALITY

Auditing is part of a quality strategy plan of an organization. After the audit when the results are reported, the findings should be used to correct problems and improve the system. When you are auditing even part of a project, you are reviewing the quality of the system.

Quality is all encompassing—everything from the work space to the last dotted I or crossed T affects the project. A messy workplace may be perceived as unorganized, not standardized, or not disciplined. Anything tested or developed there might be negated or at best questionable under those conditions. Everything matters and everything is a matter of quality. Quality is the point of the audit. By raising the quality standard you are improving the product. Make quality issues (like a messy workplace) its own part of your final report and let the company decide what it wants to do.

1.4 AUDITOR'S NOTES

I started this book to help companies that did not have written procedures or processes. A few notes:

- While auditing, reference published standards to underscore the parameters for your particular application.

- A software group with a non-documented workflow, is a ship without a chart. Your job will be to utilize the standards for the group to stay the course.

- For an internal audit to be objective, you must be independent from the group you are auditing.

- An observation is anything you see that is not against the standard. This may or may not be relevant to the overall success of the project.

- A finding is an observation that goes against the published standard (or in a non-documented project, against the best practices and normal process in the industry) and requires correction.

1.5 TYPES OF AUDITS

To understand what type of audit you are performing, you must understand the three basic types:

- System audits   • Process audits   • Product audits

Each level covers its own special area. The lowest level of audits is the product audit. This audit details the finished product. How is this product made? Is it easy to operate? Are the reports correct? As an auditor, you could run the software product with the specifications and see if they have all been met. This audit is focused on the product itself.

The next level audit is the process audit, which evaluates the methods used to verify a task and is performed the same way each time. Think of this as the production area—if a product is produced the same way each time, the results will be consistent. To improve the quality, improve the process. This is the most-performed audit because the changes at this level show quick results. This audit could include the product audit (see Figure 1.2).

Figure 1.2 Types of audits.

The highest level is the system audit (also called quality audit). This is the largest audit, and it can cover a whole company—every department down to the product. A full-scale system audit will cover all aspects of the system. System audits are to verify that quality management systems and the organizational plans are adequate and effective in meeting the company's requirements. This audit could include the process and product audits (see Figure 1.2).

There are other ways to describe audits. An internal audit is the organization auditing itself. There is also a second-party audit, in which a company will audit another company, such as a supplier. An external audit is when an outside company is hired to perform the audit.

1.6 STANDARDS

There are international, national, and industry standards that companies can use as guides. The best known are those from the International Standard Organization (ISO), which has the ISO 9000 "Quality Management Systems" series. ISO 9000-3 is *Part 3: Guide for the Application of ISO 9001 to Development, Supply, Installation and Maintenance of Computer Software.* There is also ISO 19011, *Guidelines for Quality and/or Environmental Management Systems Auditing.*

The Software Engineering Standards Committee of the IEEE Computer Society has many standards that could provide a base for an audit. Here are a few standards:

- IEEE Std 730-2002 Standard for Software Quality Assurance Plans

- IEEE Std 828-2005 Standard for Software Configuration Management Plans

- IEEE Std 829-1998 Standard for Software Test Documentation

- IEEE Std 830-1998 Recommended Practice for Software Requirements Specifications

- IEEE Std 1012-2004 Standard for Software Verification and Validation

- IEEE Std 1016.1-1993 Guide to Software Design Descriptions

- IEEE Std 1028-1997 Standard for Software Reviews

- IEEE Std 1058-1998 Standard for Software Project Management Plans

- IEEE Std 1074-1997 Standard for Developing Software Life Cycle Processes

- IEEE Std 1233-1998 Guide for Developing System Requirements Specifications

- IEEE/EIA 12207.2-1997 Standard for Information Technology

These are excellent guides and standards. There might be a contractual require-ment for the use of a standard(s). If the auditee adopts a standard you will need the standard number and the year it was released. Every few years the standards are changed, so the year of the standard is important. Sometimes during a project, a new standard comes out and the software developers decide not to work with the newer standard because they would have to rework too much. This is fine; they should stay on the same standard they started with and complete the project. Changes in midstream can be costly and may have little impact on the project. If the contract requires that a software project use the latest standard, the auditee must comply.

Be sure to check the contractual documents to see what guides or (inter)national standards are to be used during the development of the product. These standards can impact the cost and be a major factor in the development of the software.

Standards are voluntary unless contractually obligated between auditee and client.

Sometimes companies utilize a compilation from many sources and their own previous development projects. If there are no software standards or direc-tives, you will need something to guide you through the audit. You can use the spirit of the standards, meaning you cannot hold them to the letter but you can use the flow.

1.7 CAPABILITY MATURITY MODEL INTEGRATION

Capability maturity model integration (CMMI) is a process improvement maturity model for development of products and services.[4] In my opinion CMMI is the biggest and best process modeling. If the auditee company has passed a CMMI audit, they are assigned a CMMI level number. Five is the highest and one the lowest. One says that the company is developing a product. All companies start at this level But very few make it to level five.

A quick summary of the CMMI levels:

1. Processes uncontrolled, random, chaos

2. Some processes controlled, reactive

3. Processes in place; people know and follow them

4. Measuring the performance

5. Making improvement to the processes

---

[4]Mary Beth Chrissis, Mike Konrad, and Sandy Shrum, *CMMI Guidelines for Process Inte-gration and Product Improvement*, 2nd ed. (Upper Saddle River, NJ: Addison-Wesley, 2006).

If a company is in compliance with CMMI, it means that auditors have reviewed the processes and procedures and rated them equal to the level of 1–5. This audit could take months to perform. The company has to step up through the levels and it could take a year to get to the highest level. It also is a major commitment financially.

If the auditee has a CMMI level, you should audit the processes to that level. Only a registered CMMI auditor can do a CMMI audit; you are doing the audit for the client.

1.8 HIERARCHY OF STANDARDS AND REQUIREMENTS

The hierarchy is a pyramid with the company's policies and standards at the top. The company's defined area, such as the quality manual, is the second level. Below that are the procedures, which have been established by the corporation (company). The work instructions further refine the procedure into steps at the project or department level, utilizing tools, forms, and templates. When built, it looks like Figure 1.3. As you move down the pyramid, the documents cover a larger area of the business.

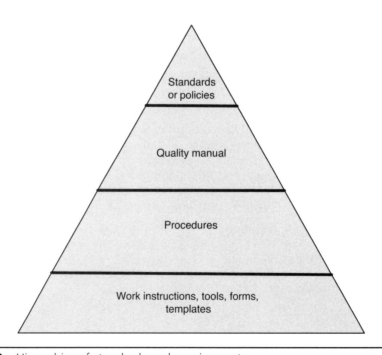

Figure 1.3   Hierarchies of standards and requirements.

Standards—The ISO 9000 family of standards represents an international consensus on good quality management practices[5] These standards are:

- ISO 9000 *Quality management systems—Fundamentals and vocabulary*

- ISO 9001 *Quality management systems—Requirements*

- ISO 9004 *Quality management systems—Guidelines for performance improvements.*

The standards have been modified for different industries. These are:

- SAE AS 9000, *Aerospace Basic Quality System Standard*

- SAE AS 9100, *Quality Systems—Aerospace—Model for Quality Assurance in Design, Development, Production, Installation, and Servicing.*

- TL 9000, *Telecom Quality Management System.*

- ISO/TS 16949, *Quality management systems—Particular requirements for the application of ISO 9001 for automotive production and relevant service part organizations*

The FDA has its own standards, for example 21 CFR Part 820, for medical.

A quality manual, according to ISO 9001, needs to reference the procedures which make up the quality management system (QMS). The quality manual is the second level down in the pyramid.

The quality manual will show any procedures that the company requires. As in AS9000, the quality might not go to the level needed to control software development.

Procedures–A procedure is a specified series of actions or operations which have to be executed in the same manner in order to always obtain the same result under the same circumstances.[6]

Note: Some companies use the term "directives" in place of procedure.

Work Instructions—A procedure does not give the detailed instructions necessary to perform the actions needed to complete the process, so the bottom level is the work instructions. These instructions fill in the gaps in the procedures. For example, the procedure might show that a back-up of a system is to be performed. The work instruction would show the files to be backed up and the location to store them.

---

[5]International Organization for Standardization, "ISO 9000 Essentials." Available from www .iso.org/iso_Catalog/management_standards/iso_9000_iso_14000/iso_9000_essentials.htm. Accessed July 6, 2009.

[6]Available from en.wikipedia.org/wiki/Procedure. Accessed March 19, 2009.

1.9 QUALITY RECORD

A quality record is any hard-copy or electronic document filed with the document name, subject, date, time, place, and who attended or performed the task. This record reports output events such as:

- Meeting minutes
- Logs
- Review minutes
- Error reports
- Worksheets

There is an old audit saying, "If it is not written down, it didn't (or won't) happen." It is important to understand that you will HEAR many things, but you need to SEE written proof or objective evidence that will verify the information. These records could be in a file drawer or on a computer. The point is they need to exist and they need to be available. Using a software package that manages documents is the best medium because it can't be modified after the fact. This is the type of record you can accept for proof of an event.

1.10 TIMELINE AND NAME GAME

We need names for different events during development. The following timeline shows the order of some events. The names used worked well with students in the System Design course I taught a few years ago. Every company has its own naming convention. I know half of you are rolling your eyes. If I used different names, the other half would be rolling their eyes. You need to pick out which of the auditee document names match the same function as shown in Figure 1.4, so the rest of this makes sense.

Allow me to paraphrase Dr. Wayne Dyer from one of his audiotape seminars: "Don't look at my finger; look at what it is pointing at." Understand that though the names may be different, their function within the document will be the same.

Figure 1.4 is a sample timeline so the distance between the milestones is not representative of a real situation. With each project, the range between the milestones will vary as your particular circumstances dictate.

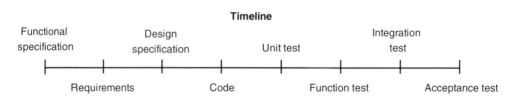

Figure 1.4   Timeline.

1.11 GENERAL AUDIT PROCESS

–Full Audit –Periodical Audit –Phase Audit

Generally there are three different audits. The first is a full audit of any function or, in our case, the project. Then there is the periodical audit done monthly, quarterly, or even yearly to ensure that the procedures are still being done correctly. One common periodical audit is configuration control because it is a major part of good software practices. There also can be an audit performed when the development goes from one phase to the next. A good example is when the project transitions from requirements to the design phase. The purpose is to show that the phase has been completed correctly and that the project is ready to move to the next phase. There is more about this in Chapter 2.

Because the periodical and phase audits are done repeatedly during the audit process, the purpose and scope are already defined. While the announcements, opening meeting, and closing meeting can be informal events, in the phase audit, presenting the report becomes a major event. If the phase audit has too many or very important findings, the company might stop the development from going to the next step. This is exactly why the audit process should be mandatory. I grew up hearing, "If its worth doing, it's worth doing well." Keep the team focused and ensure that every effort to produce the best product has been made.

Figure 1.5 shows a simple flowchart for a one-time or first-time audit that is used by most auditors. There is a brief explanation for each box. In the following chapters, I'll discuss this in greater detail.

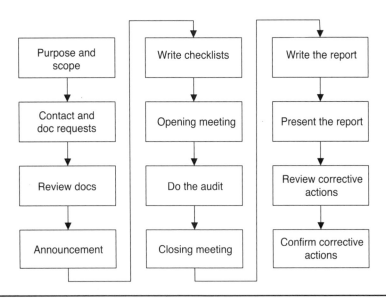

Figure 1.5   General audit process.

1.11.1 Purpose and Scope

There is a reason that the client has asked for an audit. Ask what the client is looking to learn from the audit. If you do not know, you are working at a major disadvantage. Without knowing the objective of the audit, you will need to write up everything, which will add time and raise the cost. Or. . . you will end up with a scatter effect: lots of bits of information but never honing in on the specific issue of concern to the client.

(General note: the term "client" is a person or department requesting the audit—it does not necessarily mean a customer, though it could.)

The scope is how deep into the project you need to go. How many days do you have to come up with your report? Is there a quality standard that the company works with, such as ISO 9001, or an industry or a company quality standard (like the FDA or another regulatory agency)? Under whose authority are you performing this function, and will that authority tell the auditee that you are coming? An announcement of your impending arrival to perform the audit establishes the chain of command and lets the auditee know that you're a link and answer upward. It also gives the auditee time to get their ducks in a row—always best for the most effective audit. There are more questions than answers, but this is a fraction of the information you need to know before you begin (more details in Chapter 3 The Audit's Purpose and Scope).

1.11.2 Contact and Document Requests

You need to contact the software department manager. You need to ask what documents are available, including any unfinished documents. When the manager asks (and he or she will) which documents you want, tell them to start with the organizational chart, schedule, statement of work, functional specification, design, software, interface specifications, planning documents, coding standard or guide, and any other documents supporting the project. As we've already determined, there might be different names for the documents, but the manager should understand what you need to review. Don't allow the manager to hand you alphabet soup. If he starts tell you about SOW, SDP, and IDS, ask what those stand for and write them down as a checklist for when the documents arrive. As an auditor you want to know the quality of the documents and whether any documentation steps have been skipped. The more you know about the system (project) that the auditee is developing, the more defined your questions will be (more in Chapter 3 The Audit's Purpose and Scope.)

1.11.3 Review the Documents

Now that you have the documents, you have to understand the overall purpose of the project. There is an easy way to review the documents and learn how to read them. This will be covered in Chapter 14 Reviewing Software Documents.

1.11.4 Announcement

You must give the project notice of the coming audit. Just remember that you need to review the documents. The lead time before an audit should be reasonable. It's always best to coordinate with the client. If possible, include a copy of the checklist with the announcement.

1.11.5 Writing the Checklist

The checklist is the roadmap you will to use to audit; it gives you directions for completing the scope. This is explained in Chapter 5, Conducting the Audit.

1.11.6 Opening Meeting

At this meeting you are going to tell the project manager (lead) what you will be doing (purpose and scope) and how long you think it will take. You answer any questions the manager has (Chapter 4, Opening Meeting).

1.11.7 The Audit

Where do you start, and what are the steps you need to take to find out the condition of the project? These questions are answered in the main section of this book. Know what to look for and what questions to ask (Chapters 8 to 21).

1.11.8 Closing Meeting

What is the purpose of the closing meeting, and what do you show the attendees at the meeting? What area should be covered? This is the meeting in which you tell the auditee of your findings and observations. Be sure to highlight any area that has an excellent process or procedure. At this meeting you give a general report; the details come later in the final report. More information on this is in the Closing Meeting and Final Report chapter (Chapter 6).

1.11.9 Writing the Report

The whole audit comes down to the report. The best audit ever done could be a waste of time if the facts are not conveyed to the client. How do you write the report to cover the original purpose and scope? How will you list the findings and observations of the audit? (See Chapter 6, Closing Meeting and Final Report.)

1.11.10 Present the Report to the Client

The report is finished, so what do you do with it? Who gets copies? What is included? A copy of the report goes to the client and another to the auditee. Both need to have the details of the audit so they are "on the same page." (See Chapter 6, Closing Meeting and Final Report.)

1.11.11 Review the Corrective Actions

You have made a number of findings. A group of corrective action requests are needed. These requests address the findings, and it is up to the auditee to write up what they intend to do to correct the problem(s). In this step, you are given the chance to review the ideas and make comments. This is covered in great detail in Chapter 7, Audit Follow-up and Closure.

1.11.12 Auditing Corrective Actions

You may be requested to return to the auditee site and confirm that the corrective actions have been addressed (Chapter 7, Audit Follow-up and Closure).

1.12 HOW TO USE THE QUESTIONS

In this book you will see two types of questions. The first are general questions found in the text of the paragraph. These are questions like, "Do they spend the extra money to use a queue?" or "Is there a log or database of ideas not in the requirements that have been talked about and put on hold?" They are to make a point in the paragraph.

The second type are sample questions for the audits. They sometimes run in a sequence to probe for facts. Being an auditor is not unlike being a detective. For each job, the goal is to arrive at an acceptable conclusion by eliciting information through a series of probing questions. A question might lead in two or more directions, and more questions cover those directions. If an answer is "no" or "we don't do that," the string of questions is stopped. But if the answer is "yes," there is an opportunity for more information gathering.

It is a good idea to use a spreadsheet program to write the questions. The first column is for the title of the person who will answer your question—for example, the manager or tester. Column 2 is the number of the question. Look at the example in Figure 1.6. You are basically asking the same question of two people. Write the questions in subject groups. When you are finished writing the checklist, sort the questions by job title. This lets you ask all the questions for the manager in one sitting. At the end of the audit, sort the questions by question number to regroup by subject matter to do the analysis.

Who	#	Questions
manager	1	Can a tester bring you a problem?
tester	2	Can you take a problem to your manager?

Figure 1.6 Checklist layout example.

There will be sample questions to help put the checklist together in each chapter. They are not all of the questions to be asked, but they provide a good start. At the end of the day, review the work. If an area troubles you, add questions where needed. It might take multiple questions to uncover a finding. Figure 1.7 shows another format for the sample questions.

Sometimes you just need a direction to follow, so you ask a yes/no question. In the first question in Figure 1.7, there are two answers and each would result in a different second question. The follow-up question is defined by the answer in the parentheses. If the answer is not there, skip to the next question at the higher level. In Figure 1.8, if the answer to question 1 is no, go to question 3. If the answer is yes, go to question 2, get the answer for 2, then move on to question 3.

everyone		Is the sky blue?
everyone		(Yes) Do you want to go to the beach?
everyone		(No) Is it going to rain?

Figure 1.7 Sample format.

everyone	1	Did a car just go by?
everyone	2	(Yes) Did you see who was driving?
everyone	3	Are we going in for dinner now?

Figure 1.8 Sample questions.

1.13 EXAMPLES

Sometimes I use an example to illustrate my point. When I write about a company as an example I put it in a box as in Figure 1.9. You have already seen an example in this chapter. Of course, it also lets you skip it if you already understand my point.

In these boxes I show examples from companies I have worked for or consulted with. Not all the examples are from the quality side of the house; some are witnessed working within the software world. These examples are only to help you understand some of the quality issues you might see during an audit.

Figure 1.9   Example box.

2

Software Audit Life Cycle

Timing is everything. In your personal and business life, timing could mean the difference between success and failure. In software as in all development the work runs on a time schedule. The project moves from one event to the next until the project is complete. Software uses different development models, and each has its own sequence of events.

Audits also follow a sequence of events particular to a software model. If you audit something, stay within the phase. In the beginning of the project, the auditor should look at procedures and processes that should be in place at this time. Likewise, an auditor who comes to a project near the end should not be looking at the start-up procedures. However, if a successful audit model has been developed, revisiting the procedures and processes reviewed will be of great value to the next start-up. In both cases, time and money could be wasted for no reason. Look to do the right audit at the right time.

To do an audit at the right time, you need to understand the Software Development Life Cycles (SDLC), sometimes called the System Development Life Cycles (SDLC). There are many ways to describe software life cycles. The most basic is definition, development, and maintenance. In definition we are writing the "wish list". In development we refine the wish list and bring the ides full circle to a completed product. Maintenance is following and adapting the product for continued usefulness. Further, within every life cycle exist models with specific applications.

Every company has its own model that it adjusts and adapts for each product. For example: No matter how many varieties of cookies my wife bakes, the model is the same—cream butter, add sugar, then egg and vanilla, flour goes in last. We always have a different product, but by using a familiar method (or model). There is higher efficiency and a fairly predictable outcome.

To better understand the software audit cycle, you first need a better understanding of the software audit life cycle. As an auditor, you need to know when the best time for the different audits is according to the life cycle. Understanding where the software is in the development cycle will highlight areas that need to be audited.

All questions in this chapter point at topics. The detailed questions for these topics are in other chapters.

2.1 SOFTWARE DEVELOPMENT LIFE CYCLES

Let's first look at the software development life cycles with the development models. Understanding the development models will help you to talk to the auditee. For the purpose of this book, I've elected to separate the models into two categories: primary and secondary models. Primary models are standalone or complete models. Secondary models are models that blend two or more of the primary models. There are five primary modeling approaches and a sixth that is a combination of any of the others. The primary models are:

- Waterfall

- Spiral

- Incremental

- Prototyping

- Object-oriented Programming System (OOPS)

- Blend of others

The secondary models are:

- Cleanroom

- Rapid Application Development (RAD)

- Agile

- Extreme Programming (XP)

Once a company selects a development model, it usually will customize it. Most companies do not follow any model strictly. Models are not written in concrete; every reference book puts a little different spin on them. Generally, an author writes about the particular model he has seen and used. Over my long and varied career, I've had the opportunity to work with most of these models. My intent here is to give you an overview, some basic information on each, to use as a reference point. Various models exist because this is not a "one size fits all" process. Different applications require different models. Learning the differences between the models will give the auditor a better audit knowledge base and, ultimately, a better audit.

2.1.1 The Waterfall Model

The Waterfall Model is the first and oldest model for development. In the beginning, the programmer was given a function that needed to be automated. Business programs were strung together to complete the system. As systems grew larger and more complicated, the need for a model to control development surfaced.

The waterfall name comes from the steps used to develop the system. As each step is completed, the development falls to the next step (Figure 2.1).

This classic model started it all. It was simple and easy to understand. The steps are:

Idea/Functional Specification—the "wish list" is turned into a functional specification (or requirements).

Analysis/Plan—This is the most important step. This is when the system is roughed out. Using the specifications, determine how the system needs to be built. Characteristics include:

• Databases—where and how the information is stored.

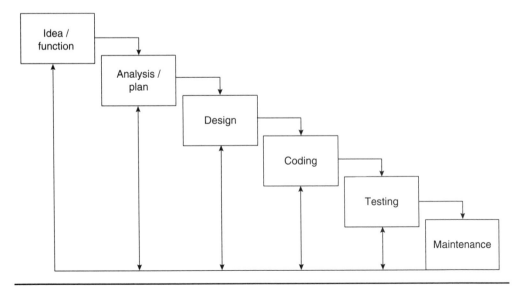

Figure 2.1   Waterfall model.

- Communications—the link between databases, servers and other computers.

- Controls—how you travel through the program(s).

- Source of inputs—how information gets into the computer— everything from credit cards, check readers, and supermarket scanners to data entry.

- Output to whom—information from the computer—everything from your credit card purchase being accepted to inventory control.

- Performance—details the speed of the information processing

- Behavior—everything from accuracy to how the software responds to input, equipment, and so on.

- Special functions—defining any special routine to handle special events.

Take all the characteristics into account before roughing out strategies and plans.

Design—In the design step, the requirements and roughed out plans are combined. What type of computer will be used? How will information be stored? Where will it be needed, and how will it get there? How will the information be entered into the system, and how will it be retrieved? What will screens look like? These are the issues for the design team.

Coding—The programmer will take the requirements and the design to write the actual code. In most cases, the system and programming are two different functions though they can overlap. Did the programmer get enough information to write the programs? Does the programmer understand the flow of the system?

Testing—Have you ever heard the term "throwing it over the wall"? It refers to the stage in the life cycle when the programmers pass the torch to the testers and offer no more support. The program needs to be tested to ensure that it works properly and to confirm that the requirements have been completed. Does the tester have a plan or test script? How much support does the programmer give the tester?

Maintenance—Fixes, changes, and upgrades will be available from time to time. How are they sent to the customers? Do programmers have to install the new software? How much time does it take to be completed? Do they need to take the system offline to do the work?

A pitfall of waterfall development is that in spite of the plans and best intentions, projects never run sequentially and there is always some new request or function the customer cannot live without. Another shortcoming is that the software is not seen until the last half of the project. Some companies will move the coding to a little earlier in the development. Additionally, in the Waterfall Model, things can be dropped into the next stage without cross talk between the phases. Be aware of these pitfalls and keep in mind that through better planning you can mitigate these shortcomings.

Planning is the biggest and most important step (or phase) of the project. Find out how much time was spent developing the plan. Most companies will speed through the planning stage to get to the design and programming. One or two skipped or poorly defined requirements can cause a failed system or cost major time and money to repair.

2.1.2 The Spiral Model

For some companies the shortcomings of the waterfall method created a need for a new model. The idea was to use the best parts of waterfall and lower the risk. The spiral model was developed to do this. The article entitled "A Spiral Model of Software Development and Enhancement" by Barry Boehm appeared in the May 1988 *IEEE Journal.* Later articles often reference the model as the spiral model or Boehm model.

Figure 2.2 is a simple form of the spiral model. The diagram is divided into four quadrants:

- Determine objectives, alternatives, and constraints

- Evaluate alternatives, identify and resolve risk

- Develop and verify next-level product

- Plan the next phase, customer reviews

The spiral starts in the upper left quadrant and close to the center. As you move around the center, the line moves toward the outside. Now take each phase of the waterfall and make a complete rotation. Each phase passes through the four quadrants. In the first quadrant, the objectives for the phase are developed. Moving (to the right) into the next quadrant, the function is evaluated and reviewed for any risks. The next (moving down) quadrant is to develop the function. The fourth quadrant (to the left) is the planning of the next phase. This could also be a review by the customer to see if the ideas have been followed. By keeping the customer in the loop, resulting feedback keeps the project on track. This maintains a high level of customer satisfaction.

As an auditor, what should you be looking at to audit this model? Is there any step (quadrants) being skipped or rubber stamped? Are the objectives clear? Are

Planning

Risk analysis

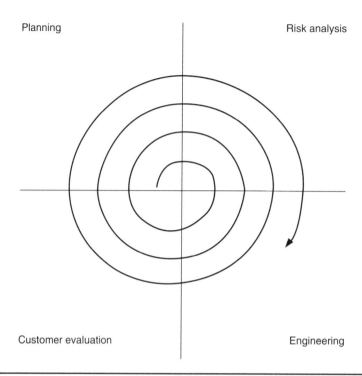

Customer evaluation

Engineering

Figure 2.2   Simple spiral model.[1]

alternatives reviewed looking for better solutions? Are the risks defined and do they have a mitigation plan developed? Was the model being followed?

Nothing is perfect, and a potential problem with this model is the customer review. If every change has to be run past the customer, think of the potential delays. Now factor in that human nature is such that most people will comment when given a chance and you find the project stuck in a never ending cycle waiting as the customer refines and refines and refines. . . .

2.1.3 The Incremental Model

Another offshoot of the Waterfall Model is the Incremental Model. It is used to divide a large project into smaller, more manageable pieces. Division allows the components to be developed while still overlapping and parallel.

Components that have not defined all the requirements can be delayed while other components can continue. Management should coordinate requirements to ensure the individual components will fit together and operate effectively.

Integration can be either simple (with each component coming in one at a time) or management's biggest nightmare. If the groups did not communicate,

---

[1]Boehm, B.W. (1983). Proceedings, Workshop on Software Maintenance. New York: IEEE Computer Society Press.

the modules will not work together. Good communication is essential to avoid redesigns or rewrites.

The natural tendency for a designer is to look at the requirements and design from the perspective of their experience. If you give 10 designers the same requirements, all of the designs will be different. Most will work. In the Incremental Model, you may have one group to output data and another to receive it. The two groups need to agree on the data, the layout, the types, and the timetable.

The main drawback with this model is the need for excellent communication and coordination between various participants. A strong management presence is a must.

2.1.4 Prototyping

Prototyping is the development of a mock-up of a product, or a simulation. If a customer wants a product developed but does not know exactly how, prototyping is a good solution.

When a customer wants something that is a new concept, but does not want to pay for a total development to find out if it works, a designer can develop a simple model of the idea, develop it, and show the customer. If after reviewing the prototype and determining whether it meets his/her original concept objectives, the customer can make an informed decision. If modifications are needed, it can go back to the designer for adjustments. See Figure 2.3.

A prototype could be completed in two days or two years. I worked on a proof of concept that ran for years. There were over 30 developers assigned, and the budget was in excess of $20 million. Sometimes prototypes work very well. . . .

While prototypes have a useful place as a model within the life cycle, a major drawback is that endless refining may never get the project off the ground.

> Many years ago a friend of mine owned a company that had a very odd way of pricing its products. They were growing and knew they needed to be computerized for greater efficiency. I spent an entire day with their pricing person, then went home and created a mock-up of their pricing system. I did the demo and they ended up ordering an entire custom invoice and accounts receivable system.

The prototyping model loosely follows a spiral model. It differs in that it only works on a mock-up.

Work usually starts off with the concept of what is to be done and moves into the design. Once the design is formed, work moves into the building part. In software, this could be the writing of a program or many modules. The company can

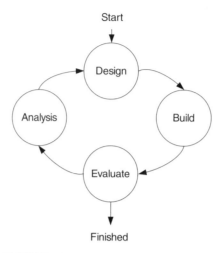

Start

Design

Analysis

Build

Evaluate

Finished

Figure 2.3   Prototyping model.

then evaluate the results, leading up to analyzing how the system can be improved. Work continues around this circle until the evaluation shows there are no more improvements to be made and customer satisfaction has been attained. NOTE: In this model, customer satisfaction can also be disapproving of a concept.

2.1.5 The Object-Oriented Programming System (OOPS)

The Object-Oriented Programming System is "[p]rogramming languages in which independent objects perform specific tasks. The objects work together by passing messages to each other to invoke specific actions. The key features of Object-Oriented Programming are message passing, encapsulation, and inheritance"[2]

"Object-Oriented modeling methods combine data modeling and procedure modeling into one modeling method."[3]

In the continuing search for a better development model, Object-oriented (OO) is the latest model. It had a very rough start in the 1990s. Many companies started developing in the object-oriented model before they completely understood it and failed. It took years of trial and error with the results being published, so that others could build on the results. Now it is the strongest and most-used development method.

The three advantages in using OO are breaking the system into components called objects, designing objects to be reusable, and a powerful data model. Sys-

---

[2]Len Fertuck, *System Analysis & Design with Modern Methods* (Dubuque, IA: B&E Tech, 1995), p. 640.
[3]Michael Gibson and Cary Hughes, *Systems Analysis and Design: A Comprehensive Methodology with Case* (Danvers, MA: Boyd & Fraser Publishing Company, 1994), p. 87.

tems developed using OO are usually easier to maintain and are more flexible. Reusable objects cut development cost.

A major drawback is that managing a large volume of reusable code—storage, cataloging, and making it available to other programmers—sometime decreases the cost benefit of reuse.

2.1.6 Blending of Models (or Hybrid)

We've seen models develop as an evolutionary process; for example, Spiral is based on Waterfall. Blending of models takes the parts of a model and adapts them to fill a particular niche in the life cycle in use within a company. The benefits, of course, are they get a perfect fit. The downside is that they need to ride shotgun on the weaknesses to prevent failure of the model. The most important point to take away from this section is this: If you are auditing a hybrid model, then blend your audit. Be sure your methods reflect this unique model.

When a blend is used by more than one company, they sometimes get their own name. Here are a few examples of such well known blends.

2.1.7 Cleanroom

The focus of the cleanroom process is to prevent defects before they get into the project. They are being proactive rather than reactive.

2.1.8 Rapid Application Development

This prototyping model does not waste time on lengthy planning schedules. It gets right to work and limits those endless refinements of the spiral model of thinkers.

Introduced by James Martin, the rapid application development (RAD) methodology involves iterative development and the construction of prototypes.[4] Audit this the same way you would audit iterative development and prototypes.

2.1.9 Agile

This method divides the work into small sections that are then put through a full development cycle by a small team whose emphasis is on communication and an effective joint effort.

---

[4]Available from http://en.wikipedia.org/wiki/rapid_application_development. Accessed August 13, 2008.

2.1.10 Extreme Programming

This is a high-intensity, full-throttle, in-depth, time-boxed approach to improving software quality.

2.2 HOW AUDITS FIT INTO THE LIFE CYCLE

Audits are an integral part of software quality. Knowing what part of the development process on which to do the audit is key. As the auditor, you need to know the model they are using and what phase of the model they are in.

My golden rule of auditing is that the audit must help the auditee or the client. The information gleaned from the audit process must be used for project status and action. Even if the audit has big findings, the auditee can move to fix the problems.

As we learned in Chapter 1, there are three types of audits: system, process, and product. The system audit is the highest order, encompassing all that's needed during the research and development life cycle.

To create and develop the model for the audit, we first need to look at these elements and understand their importance in the hierarchy of software life cycle auditing. Those who would jump to the conclusion that the all-encompassing system is the focus of any new endeavor would be wrong.

In the beginning there is a concept, which is the product. All effort and focus is directed at defining the requirement and functional specifications that will result in the product. See Figure 2.4. At this point in the process, the product is at the top of the triangle because it's getting all the attention.

The need for procedures and the system is recognized but not yet defined, so they are at the base—part of the picture, but not in the focus position at the top. While product is still on top, plans are in progress and analysis of these plans is redefining the order. Procedures are the result and they now begin to rival product in importance. As design and coding progress and move into test-

System
Process
Product

Figure 2.4 Focus for a new product.

ing, the system begins to come up and equals the importance of the product and procedure. This is a more balanced base, with all three sharing equally in what is the ultimate goal of customer satisfaction, as illustrated in the product pyramid in Figure 2.5.

Utilizing the Waterfall Model, since it is the common thread running through all the development models, we will be able to see how and where the audit fits into the software development life cycle. Audits can take place during a phase or when you are stepping from one phase to the next (remember the throwing it over the wall reference?). These phase changes are often called "gates."

Now we will take the Product Triangle and make it a Product Pyramid. The height of the pyramid would be the percentage of completion of the project. In a perfect world, the center of the pyramid would rise with all three elements being equal. Figure 2.5 shows a completed project having all three elements completed.

Here are the waterfall phases we will use, with one additional step. The proof of concept has been added because more and more projects have to show how the idea will work before companies will fund them:

- Proof of concept (or demo)—possibly a prototype

- Idea/Functional specification

- Analysis/Planning

- Designing

- Coding

- Testing

- Maintenance

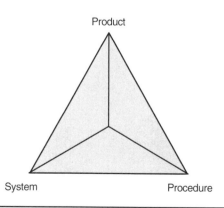

Figure 2.5 Product triangle.

2.2.1 Proof of Concept (or Demo)

2.2.1.1 Phase for Proof of Concept

Proof of concept is taking an idea and investigating to see if the idea has merit.

Recently I took my car in for service because my transmission was slipping. The technician told me that he would load a new version of the software that runs my transmission, and it should fix the problem. Wow! A completely electronically controlled transmission.

At some point, this was just an idea, but auto industry engineers had to do a feasibility study. Was the idea practical? Did the necessary parts exist or could something be adapted? What about the cost involved in design and production? Perhaps a prototype was ordered. What's important here is that innovation is born from a concept that has been examined and determined to have merit.

This is a rough outline of proof of concept. If the company has a department that handles the proof of concept projects, there is a system and procedure in place for development. An auditor can come into this department to perform system and procedures audits.

If a team is put together to develop the proof of concept project, all of the work concentrates on the product. There will be no system or procedures worked on during this period. Everything outside of the product will cost additional money, and the argument is why develop systems and procedures if the product might never get off the drawing board. Two things come into play at this point. The first is determining whether the team that developed the proof of concept is the team that will do the development. The second point is the amount of time between the completion of the proof of concept and the actual start of development.

In either case, documentation is crucial. If a different development team is chosen, documentation sometimes becomes the only record of what the proof of concept study endorsed. A new team might try to design its own solution to the problem and create expensive delays. If the development team cannot talk to the original team, details are lost. If approval takes a long time, details are forgotten. In the transmission example, there had to be information about the particular part that was being designed. An audit should be performed at the end of the proof of concept phase to evaluate the records and documentation. The audit became more critical as time grew longer between the proposal and the start of development.

2.2.1.2 Gate for Proof of Concept

Here are some questions to ask at this gate:

		Is there a copy of the original agreement for this phase?

		Is there a list of objectives for this project?
		What documents have been created from this project?
		If the project is not continued, what have you learned?
		How is the lesson learned from this project documented?
		Is a preliminary budget laid out?
		How long is this budget good? Is there an expiration date?
		Is a preliminary schedule outlined?
		Are preliminary personnel requirements listed?
		Are all the findings documented?
		Are the failures documented?
		Are copies of the budget and actual costs recorded?
		Is new equipment required?
		Has equipment been purchased for this project?
		Where will it be stored?
		Is special software purchased for this project?
		Where are the licenses and installation disk being stored?
		Have all the files and programs been backed up?
		What documents have been saved?
		Are the documents complete?
		Have the documents been reviewed?
		Has the manager of development signed them?
		Does each document align with other documents?
		Are there suggestions from the team for the next team?
		How is the project being reported to the customer?
		Is there a presentation?
		May I have a copy of the presentation?

		When and to whom are you presenting?
		What's next?

2.2.2 Idea/Functional Specification

2.2.2.1 Phase for Idea/Functional Specification

The idea has become a product through the proof of concept process or by going directly to development. In the beginning, the idea is expanding and functions or requirements are written, modified, and rewritten. People add their thoughts during meetings. Some are added to the product and others are dropped. Everyone has heard, "Wouldn't it be nice to do *blank.*" The product requirements become an entity of their own.

Nowhere in the preceding paragraph are the words *system* or *procedure* written. All of the focus is on the product. The Product Pyramid becomes distorted only by the product being developed. The only system and procedures used are what the company has already in place. These might only be the high-level general procedures.

How much time should you as the auditor spend on each element? Should the auditor come with a 10-page checklist on procedures at this point? No. The auditor should concentrate on the product with only a few questions on procedures.

At the end of this phase, the functional specification or requirements should be at least 80 percent complete. You know there will be changes during the rest of the development. Where should you, the auditor, be looking next? Configuration control of the specification should be the first thing checked. Is there version control (is everyone working from the most recent copy?) or is there just a document being passed around?

Is there a log or database of ideas for future versions not in the requirements? Many ideas are lost at this point in the project. If the designer knows what is coming in future releases, he can plan for it and avoid redesigns. How many reviews were performed on the specification before it was completed? Were notes and problems listed in the minutes? Were they all completed? Were all the right people included in the reviews? Who are the right people? Was this phase rushed or was an adequate amount of time allotted to writing the best specification? Was any risk noted? If so, was it fully documented?

If it is important enough to be audited at this point, take the requirements apart. Group the requirements into individual functions. You are from the outside, not part of the inner circle that put the requirements together. See if you can figure out each function—what it does and how it does it. It might take hours, but it is well worth it if you find holes or conflicting requirements.

2.2.2.2 Gate for Idea/Functional Specification

Planning is what needs to be done to complete the project. No planning means no project or a very costly project. A well-planned project will have minimum problems. Some of these plans should at least be started. Your list of plans might include:

- Software development plan
- Quality plan
- Configuration control plan
- Test plan
- Integration plan
- Project control plan
- Environmental plan

Other items to audit before the completion of the functional specification phase are:

- Sales/purchase orders
- Statement of work
- Any preliminary system requirements
- Internal documents used to develop the quote
- Any type of schedule developed
- Software risk reports
- Hardware and personnel resource plans
- Space and other administration report/plans

Here are some questions for software development:

		What software risks are there?
		Is the software risk rated?
		What will be done to lower the software risk?
		What software opportunities will there be?
		Is the technology new and will it help the company?
		Will the software or part of it be reused on another project?

		Who will own the software and rights at the end of the project?
		Will the company be licensing the software? Annual charge?
		What configuration control system will you use?
		What are you doing for a quality system?
		How often will the software get audited?
		What are the plans for reviews, peer reviews, and software walk-through?
		Will quality be monitored? How?
		What manpower is needed?
		What special needs will the employees have?
		Will you need to hire special talent?
		Can an employee be trained to do the job?
		What degree of training will be needed?
		Define the timing limits.
		Define preliminary volume limits, memory, disk, processor, speed.
		Is the software going to be scalable?
		What standards must be enforced?
		Is there a special standard such as FDA, FAA, IEEE, or ISO?
		Are the parts of the standards defined?
		Define any safety issues.
		How will you minimize the safety issues?
		Will you be upgrading the system periodically?
		Do you have a high-level block diagram (10,000 feet)?
		What special equipment (test or other) will be needed?
		What kind of maintainability will be needed?
		Will updates be on the Internet or on CDs?

		Will you lock down the contract with all the requirements?
		Will you define all deliverables and milestones?
		Is there any charge back on missed milestones?

These questions need not be answered sequentially. But they must be answered, especially the questions that can affect the pricing. If these are not answered, the project could have major cost overruns. Here are the cost questions:

		Is there enough floor space for the development?
		Is there enough lab space?
		Do you have the team or project manager?
		Is there a flat cost figure for each skill set needed?
		What is the initial equipment cost? PCs, servers, and so on.
		Will the project need the newest equipment at a premium price?
		How much support personnel will be needed?
		Will special equipment need to be designed and built?
		Will a user's manual be required?
		Will a maintenance manual be required?
		Will a service or administration manual be required?

Just defining what approach will be used in development could make a difference to the cost and to the delivery process.

Before the next phase starts, you need almost all of these questions answered. If the answers for a few questions have been narrowed down to a few options, the project might be able to start the next phase. However, shortly after the next phase starts, the answers are needed.

2.2.3 Analysis/Planning

2.2.3.1 Phase for Analysis/Planning

Here is the most important part of the whole project. Spend adequate time on the analysis and planning of the project to ensure the best possible outcome. A mistake here could cost tens or hundreds of thousands of dollars later on in the project. A lot of companies fly through this phase without doing all their homework and later will complain that the planning was not complete.

The functional specifications should be peer reviewed. A rough outline should be put together just to get a better understanding of the system. There should be a working group that includes users, software maintenance people, operators, system analysts, database programmers, and others who will be impacted by the system later on. This group should come up with at least three approaches to developing this product. The approaches should each be studied to see which is the most valid for this project.

After the approach has been selected, many plans need to be put together. These plans include:

- Software development plan
- Rough schedule
- Suppliers plan
- Type of equipment to be developed on
- Personnel qualifications
- Office space needed
- Development network plan

- Laboratory space
- Configuration management plan
- Software quality plan
- Test plan

- Budget review and update
- Installation and updates plan
- Maintenance plan

The writing of these plans starts to bring more process and system into the development. The product is still the main focus, but its prominence is ebbing as emphasis shifts to systems.

As an auditor, you need to review all of these plans. It is possible that a lot of these plans have been rolled into the software development plan. Make sure that all the subjects have been covered and documented. Also, make certain that everything from the start of development to the maintenance of the system has been taken into consideration.

2.2.3.2 Gate for Analysis/Planning

This may be the easiest or the hardest phase. As my wife said about our daughter's wedding, "It's all about the details." It will be easier if the company receives a detailed statement of work outlining the customer expectations and specifications. Things are a lot more difficult if the customer is vague and/or generalizing.

Documents you should receive and review include:

- Internal design plan
- Requirements specification

- Development plan (could be in next phase also)
- Copies of the peer review minutes

Most computer systems that you will encounter during your audits will be PC based. The following questions are from that perspective:

		Is there a simple system layout?
		Do you know how many PCs will be connected to the system?
		Are the PCs' properties defined? Speed? Memory? Disk size? Monitor size?
		Will the system use a server?
		Are the server properties defined? Speed? Memory size?
		Will the server disk be a mirror, an array, or something else?
		Will there be more than one server?
		Is there a preliminary distribution of files?
		Is there a preliminary estimate of files to be accessed?
		Is there a preliminary estimate of record sizes?
		How many layers will be used in the server?
		Will the access be directly to the database?
		Will there be queuing of data for input?
		Will the system use a database management system (DBMS)?
		Will you use third-party DBMS?
		How will you select a DBMS?
		Will any special development tools be needed?
		Will there be passwords on the database or server?
		Will the user gain access through the Internet?
		Is there a firewall already in the company?
		Will the system need a new firewall?
		Will the system use bar scanners? Hand scanners?
		Will the PCs need a touch screen?

		Will the system use a handheld device?
		Will there be daily, weekly, or monthly reports?

The requirements are the details that explain the actual system. Large requirements should be divided into smaller increments. There should be no givens; assume nothing. The person who is going to use the system does not have a computer background, and the designer does not usually have knowledge of the user's business.

At this point, we are getting to the end of the planning phase. However, the project cannot move into design until the following set of questions have been satisfactorily answered. A negative response at this point may halt progress and delay design. Ask the questions and let them defend them:

		How complete is the requirement document?
		Are there any areas that have not been defined?
		Are you waiting for more information in any area?
		Have the requirements been divided into smaller increments?
		Has the customer been part of the requirement development?
		Has the customer reviewed the requirements?
		Are all of the requirements clear?
		Are the requirements testable or measurable?
		Are any performance requirements defined?
		Do the performance numbers work with the architecture?
		Is the number of programs defined?
		Is the function of each program defined?
		Was a presentation done?
		Were the requirements clearly stated during the presentation?
		Did the speaker seem to be well prepared?
		Are there any open or skipped areas?
		Is there an estimate of the programming time line?

		Is there an estimate on how many lines of code?
		Any special tools needed for development?
		Has a software language been selected?
		Does auditee have the software language package?
		Will other software packages be needed? (word processing, spreadsheet, report writer, presentation, math, statistical)

For further information on software requirements, check out the following sources:

- Technical Report ISO/IEC TR 19759. (Chapter 2 is Software Requirements).

- IEEE std. 830-1998. Recommended Practices for Software Requirement Specifications

Don't overlook the importance of the following questions. Otherwise the project will be pushed forward into the next phase, Design, without appropriate authorization:

		Has the customer signed off the requirements?
		Has the development management signed off?
		Did the test manager sign off?
		Has marketing signed off?

2.2.4 Software Design

2.2.4.1 Phase for Software Design

Designing is not a one-man operation. All interested parties optimally (programmers, testers, users, customers, and maintenance) should be involved. As part of the design review, you should find out who was involved and their area of expertise. This information should be available in the minutes. There might not be an internal expert, so check if they used a consultant or even the customer to get the data they needed.

Design doesn't just happen. It's the result of many hours of hashing out ideas and details. Hundreds, if not thousands, of decisions need to be made during design. Each decision could affect the outcome of the system. Every variation from the original design could cause a time delay and a rewrite at the end of the project. No one likes cost overruns, so they should stay the course.

If the system has a robust design, problems will be at a minimum. A balance here must be considered. Cost versus robustness is a major factor in design. An example at this point might demonstrate the balance. Let's assume the performance specification has a requirement for the system to be able to store 200 records a minute. That's an easy number; most systems can handle it with no problem. Here are the choices: (1) Do you store directly to the database, or (2) do you queue up each record before storing it? The record would fall straight through the queue and be stored. If the system ever grows larger than 200 records, you might need queuing to keep the system running. The question: Does the company spend the extra money at the onset to build a queue?

Now let's assume the system is developed and installed. The actual count of records stored is 300 per minute. The system handles the higher number with no problems with either of the options. However, the company is doing well enough to expand into another city. Now the system is peaking at 1000 records per minute. If a queue was in place the system would keep running through peak times. Here's the question again: Does the company spend the extra money to use a queue? If they could know the future, the answer might be different at this point. A good design system will be prepared and take into account that the company will expand or grow. The system must handle the needs of a company for five or more years. Was the growth of the company in the design equation, or were only the present needs met?

Traditionally, the requirements will include the planned growth of a new system. If by chance there is no such requirement and the system is transactional, question the auditee about expectations of growth. To assist you with the auditee, you might have a software engineer calculate how much more the system can handle. Frequently, the gap between what the system can handle and the customer's growth projection happens when the design is completed too quickly.

Interfaces are also often overlooked. The design should show the types of communications to be used, such as Internet, closed system, interprocessors, suppliers' software, and many others. Needed is a map (or diagram) and what data will be transferred. At this point, lists of the data with some notes might work, or a full data dictionary might be needed. If there is no document to define the fields, in three months when the programmer needs it, no one will remember how the fields were used.

As the processes start to gel, the process portion of the Product Pyramid becomes more prominent. Focus always remains on the product, but now processes demand more time.

Peer reviews are an important part of the design development. All of the in-house experts should be invited, as well as experts you can conference with by phone. Minutes and findings should be recorded. Ask for the peer review minutes and findings, plus the documentation of the resolution of the findings. Chapter 15, on Peer Reviews, provides more details.

Review the diagrams of the system. There must be documents showing the design because they are the map to the future of the project. If the project is not documented, auditing it will be like shooting at a moving target.

Here is a checklist of things that should be happening:

- The development system has been identified.

- Development tools have been selected (operating system, compiler, and so on).

- All equipment and tools are ordered.

- Office and laboratory space is allocated.

- Manpower requirements are established.

- Updated budget.

- Development support is planned.

- List of parts to be supplied from suppliers is prepared.

- Long list of suppliers (shorten during selection) is prepared.

- How the system will be installed is decided.

- Field support of product is determined.

- Maintenance plan (after it is installed) is prepared.

2.2.4.2 Gate for Software Design

The product could be as simple as one program or as complicated as a hundred programs. When the project comes out of this phase, the design should be finalized and approved. Of course, there will be minor changes when the software code is being written.

Reviewing the product design should give you a picture of what the product will do without seeing it on a screen. This phase has brought the product into focus. A list of all the programs needed to build the system should be defined and include a description.

The presentation should start with an overview of the design diagram. The more detailed diagrams should follow. There are many detail diagrams that can be used—from simple flowcharts to object-oriented diagrams. Depending on the designers and their backgrounds, the choice of design diagram could be one of many different approaches. Here are a few:

- Top-down Method

- Entity/Relationship Modeling Method

- Function Decomposition Modeling Method

- Data Flow Diagrams
- Process Dependency Diagrams
- Program Flowcharts
- Pseudo-code
- Prototyping
- Action Diagrams
- Object-Oriented Modeling Methods
- Object-Oriented Views
- Object-Oriented Analysis and Design
- Computer-Aided Software Engineering (CASE)

This is the short list. There are many more. Whether one method is better than another is not the auditor's call. Understanding the project is the objective and the design should be left to those in that area of expertise.

Documents you should receive and review include:

- Detailed design documents
- Development plans
- Product description
- Any method documents and/or diagrams listed
- Any other document that was used to develop the design

The following is a list of questions to be answered during the gate:

		Did you receive all diagrams and documents before the review?
		Did you have enough time to review the diagrams and documents?
		Is the overview self-explanatory?
		Was a list of all programs with description provided?
		Was the top-level diagram explained properly?
		Could you, the auditor, explain the system using the overview?
		When presenting the detailed diagrams, was the most important first?

		Is each program/module explained clearly?
		Are any programs/modules missing?
		Is there an estimate on input and output data?
		Is there an estimate on database reads/writes?
		Is there a growth estimate for one, two, five years?
		What would be the effects of the growth?
		Are there estimates on processor usage?
		Will there be access levels to the system?
		Are the access levels explained?
		Will there be a monitoring program to report statistical data?
		Is there a configuration file?
		Will there be peak times for the system, and what will be the results?
		Does any data need extra security?
		Will a training class be developed during development?
		Is there an estimate of lines of code for each program?
		Are there programmers in place to do the coding?
		Are all needed resources in place?
		What is the estimate for completion of the coding and unit testing?
		Is special equipment defined?
		Is development going to be on the company's WAN/LAN?
		When can the test and case writing start?
		Is the configuration system in place?
		Are all programmers trained on the configuration system?
		Is all the development software loaded on everyone's computer?

		Is the lab space clear and available?
		How many peer reviews has the team had?
		What type of peer reviews?
		Do you have interface specifications?
		Is the schema (file, record, and field layouts) for the database defined?
		Do you, the auditor, have a copy of the schema?
		Is the security designed for Internet accessibility?

If during your audit you are not comfortable about what you see or hear, it is your job to probe. Ferreting out problems now will save time and money later and ensure a higher level of quality.

2.2.5 Coding (and Unit Testing)

2.2.5.1 Phase for Coding (and Unit Testing)

At last the designer hands off the system design to the programmers. Depending on how detailed the design, the programmer might need to design the individual programs. For example: the designer might have designed the screen layouts, colors, and maybe the feel of the programs. The programs behind the screens are designed by the programmer.

If there are strict controls, the programmer might need to design the flow of the program or maybe the interaction with other programs or databases. If there are any communications between program modules or databases, they must be defined. The programmer must understand the coding standards the department requires to write the code.

When you audit this phase, you will need to see the department process for design to determine that all programmers work in the same direction. Are the programmers talking to the database designer or programmers? Are interactive modules planned by the team? Unless there is cooperation and communication, they are courting disaster at integration.

Many peer reviews can take place during coding, such as:

- Design reviews

- Code reviews

- Interface or communication reviews

- Unit test plan reviews

Do the programmers have a unit test plan that covers all the variables for the routine or do they wing it? An error in coding at this point can be hard to find during integration testing. If the routine is handling an exception (that is, handling a communication error) the problem might not surface until it is in the field. If there is a communications problem, does everyone involved work together to find a solution?

Here is a checklist of things that should be happening:

- Are interface or communication specifications written?
- Does the test area have equipment ready?
- Are there enough programmers to complete the project on time?
- Does the schedule reflect the manpower available?
- Does all the development equipment have the same operating system?
- Are the operating systems configured the same?
- Are notes being taken for operator instruction?
- Do suppliers have the design?
- How does the project let suppliers know when there is a problem?
- Do the suppliers have a contact to answer their questions?
- Do you have the suppliers' schedule(s)?
- How are suppliers delivering their product?

At this time, any open items from the other phases leading up to coding must be checked and closed.

During coding, the Product Pyramid product leg growth slows down and the process leg continues to grow. There are few changes to the product after the design is completed, just fine tuning. This is the longest phase, so the process should be strong and in place now. At this point, product, system, and quality are pretty much equal.

2.2.5.2 Gate for Coding (and Unit Testing)

Coding is the main function of the development process. This is where all the planning comes together. Non-specific requirements will become apparent during coding. The programmers must have a direct relationship with the designers and the customer.

There is a fine line between Phase 4 and 5. As soon as software has started, integration should be receiving copies for testing. If the working relationship between the programmers and the integrators (testers) is good, the integration time will be reduced. The following questions are from the coding side, but if the integration has started, you might want to include questions from Phase 6:

		Is there a formal procedure for changing requirements?
		Does the customer approve requirement changes?
		Can additional requirements be added for clarification?
		Are you using a coding standard or guide?
		Which coding standard or guide?
		Are you using a team guide?
		Will you be using a routine header?
		(No) Why not?
		(Yes) Are you recording the history of changes?
		Do you define each routine with input and output?
		Are you allowing more than one exit in routines?
		Do you use copyright statements?
		How much of the code is commented?
		Are there comments that explain math formulas or models?
		Are there comments explaining unusual routines?
		Are you using a configuration or version control system?
		Which control system are you using?
		Has the system been baselined?
		Are you recording corrective action reports?
		How many reports do you have presently?
		Do you run any kind of code analyzer against the code?
		What is the name of the product you use?
		Will you use a code coverage product?
		Are you using any debug tools or special hardware?

		How many code reviews has the team had?
		Are you employing other types of peer reviews?
		Is the integration system built and ready?
		Do the programmers have unit test scripts or checklists?
		Have the integration people (testers) completed the test scripts?
		Is the test description document completed?
		Is the test plan completed?
		When programmers complete the programs, do they hand off to the testers?
		Has a test database been populated?
		Do the programmers and testers work as a team?
		Do the problem reports have enough information?
		Can the programmer work using the problem report only?
		Have any major design changes been necessary?
		Is there a company/project screen standard?
		Is there a color standard for screens?
		Has the team worked with the user for the screen landscape?
		Are there standards for reports/statements?
		Was a program developed to transfer data from the old database to the new database?
		Have all the programs been completed?
		Have the programs all been sent to integration?

2.2.6 Test (System Integration)

2.2.6.1 Phase for Test (System Integration)

This phase should be started before the code phase has ended. In Waterfall development, the coding phase ends and the testing begins. This is called "throwing the code over the wall." This creates a nonsupported testing environment.

With overlapping, it is more productive. The tester can take problems back to the programmer, who might still be working on the same code.

Integration needs to be planned. This is where all the parts come together to form a system. Poor planning costs time and blows the budget. It doesn't matter if each program will run independently; it's what happens when they come together. They must be able to communicate with each other. You will find more detail in the chapter about testing (Chapter 21).

As the auditor, you want to see the plan and the resources to be used. The test plan should be started from the beginning each time a fix has been made to the system. Watch for the testers, they might start up from where they found the problem. When all the testing is completed, will the testers run the whole test for an independent person for one last look at the software? A second set of eyes should run the test from the beginning, looking for anything that might have been overlooked. They need someone to ask, "Why?"

Some waterfall models show customer acceptance testing at this point. This book covers this type of testing in Chapter 21.

2.2.6.2 Gate for Test (System Integration)

System Integration can take as much as or more time than writing the code. This is the point where all the components come together and work . . . in a perfect world. It is a good concept, but not very practical. Of all testing performed on software, integration should be the most controlled. It must be planned and documented to be complete. Hit and miss has no place in the integration process.

Documents to receive and review include:

- Test plan
- Updated test description
- Test scripts/cases
- Test results
- Acceptance test script
- Copies of problem reports with conclusions
- Validation and verification documentation
- Verification checklist or script

		Were you able to start integration before all the programs were completed?
		How many test stations have you set up?
		Do you have a snapshot of the database?
		Did you maintain a test log?
		Is the configuration under control with no changes unless approved?

		Is the software tested on an approved list of operating systems?
		Have all screens sizes and resolutions been tested?
		What type of server operating system is the system using and why?
		What type of regression testing was used?
		Was an automated regression tester used?
		After a software bug was repaired or fixed, were the tests rerun?
		How often do you start from the beginning to test the system?
		Who is allowed to clear or close a problem report?
		Were the test results dated and signed?
		How many corrective action requests have been made?

Independent validation and verification (V&V) should be an ongoing process. It begins during the requirements phase and continues through integration testing:

		Is there a validation matrix or another document?
		Who performed the V&V task?
		Are they independent of the project?
		Can each task be tracked from requirement to testing?
		Has the verification list been made independently?
		Are results calculated before running the system?
		Is each requirement checked off the verification list?

2.2.7 Maintenance (Production and Deployment)

2.2.7.1 Phase for Maintenance (Production and Deployment)

The maintenance after the project is shipped must also be planned. All of the installation and update material should be in place. How the company will receive and handle problems from the field must be described. Will the customer need to buy updates or upgrades? Is the company going to sell maintenance agreements?

To audit maintenance, you should look at how the customers are being supported. How are they reporting problems with the system? Is there a help desk that customers call? If an auditee has a help desk, it would be a good idea to test it by calling with a problem. There are customers who will not buy a software product from a company because the help (or call) representative does not offer real assistance or is surly. This is something I will never understand. Why spend upward of 50 percent of the sales price to market the product and allow a person making $10 an hour to lose the next sale? I report it when I find it. Review some tapes of the service center if possible. You select the date and a few different stations to get a good feel of the type of work being done.

If the system is completely custom (a one-time sale), the maintenance of the system should have been covered in the requirements. Who is responsible for what? How does the customer request service? What kind of data does a customer need to include? Does the customer have a direct line to development?

How fast does the development company respond? How long before someone is sent to the customer's site? Is there a phone or Internet connection the development company can use to fix the problem? How long is development going to repair problems: five years, 10 years, or until the system is replaced? In many cases maintenance is not discussed during the sale. However, each side will have its own ideas on how things will be handled. If their ideas don't match, what do they do?

Look into the number and types of calls. A free update could save the company more money than a large staffed call center. Look at the number of service calls made by service people. The company should be using all this information for the next product. Tossing it into a wastebasket, or filing it in a call center's file cabinet, is wasting an opportunity to improve your customer service and further the business.

2.2.7.2 Gate for Maintenance (Production and Deployment)

This phase is the final pre-shipping countdown. Without this phase being complete, no finished product could be sent to the customer. Testing in the development labs is called alpha testing. When the first customer(s) get the product it is called beta testing. Beta testing is covered in the second set of questions:

		How will the software be sent to the customer?
		Is the software included inside a product?
		Is the software downloaded from the Internet?
		Can the software be purchased over the Internet?

		Do you have a free trial period?
		How do you control the free trial period?
		Is the software on a CD/DVD or other media?
		Will development people or field reps install the software?
		Will development people or field reps configure the system?
		Can the customer install the system?
		Is there an install program used?
		Was the install program tested?
		Does the software have a serial number?
		Is there password protection?
		Is the company (development) tracking all installations?
		How long is the guarantee for on-site or phone support?
		Are there maintenance contracts?
		Are there different levels of maintenance contracts?
		How will you stop other companies from getting your software?
		Are you selling this software by license?
		Will there be floating licenses on the server?
		If the customer goes over its licensed usage, how will you know?
		How will you handle updates?
		Downloads?
		CD/DVD?
		Will you automatically send updates to the customer?
		Will you have a Web site for Q & A or downloading?
		Will you track the companies hitting the Web site for illegal copies?
		Are all manuals completed?

		Will the customer need to get training?
		Will the training be at the customer site or your training center?
		Will the system need an administrator?
		Will the administrator need extra training?
		What kind of feedback will you get from the system?

Beta site testing is different from just sending the software to one customer. It is a study of the system in the field. All feedback is captured and reviewed. This feedback could range from the color of a screen to a major function not working correctly. The proactive way to run a beta test would be to send out the software and then contact each beta site at least once a week either individually or on a conference call with all beta sites. Of course, the beta sites would have one contact at the auditee in case any problems surface. Some development companies will tell the beta sites if a problem has been found. Letting the beta sites in on a problem inspires confidence that the auditee is on top of their game. The customer feels they have spent their money well.

Beta testing questions include:

		How many beta sites will the company use?
		What does the beta site company receive for its help?
		Does the beta site get the latest software weekly, monthly, or as needed?
		Does the beta site have a contact in the development team, and vice versa?
		Is there weekly contact with the beta sites?
		Is a status report developed each week?
		Who receives a copy of the status report?
		Is there a time limit to the beta testing?
		Is there a log on each beta site?
		Does development know the configuration at each beta site? (show)
		What is the planned time between updates to the beta sites?

Any comments or problems reported by the beta sites must be recorded and tracked. A small comment mentioned by several sites could be the difference between a quality system and an "it will do" product.

Part II

Audit Activities

3

The Audit's Purpose and Scope

In "audit" books, purpose and scope are covered in one or two paragraphs. These subjects need greater detail during software audits. For a better outcome, you and the client must agree on the purpose and scope.

Software development is a business function. There are many ways to look at it, such as think tank, new product development, support, or maintenance for ideas. In big software departments, you can find all or most of these. This leads us to the types of audits your client might need you to perform.

The purpose could be to learn why the project is a month behind schedule, why the cost is 50 percent higher than expected, what needs to be done so that the system matches an industry regulation, or simply how costs can be cut. The client will tell you what it wants from the audit. The client wants you to audit, review, or evaluate the software project. You must first understand the ground rules.

Your client could be looking into buying or investing in a company that has a great software product. The company is turning a profit, and there looks to be a major breakthrough. This is the hardest audit; every detail must be turned inside out. No details can be overlooked; all findings and observations, no matter how trivial, must be written up. Sometimes groups of findings could surface as a show stopper.

A company that was a leader in its industry went on the market to be sold. The buyer (client) asked for a full software audit. It seems that the software was written for DOS (disk operating system), and the buyer was moving to Microsoft Windows XP. The developers made all the right statements about the upgrade plan and the work was moving along nicely. During the audit, errors were revealed that would require most of the software to be rewritten. The price was renegotiated.

Another company acquired a firm that fit into its product line. The buying company announced that the division I worked for was getting the software team. No one even had a chance to look at the software. The hardware was perfect, but the software did not seem to be controlled and they didn't know what was in the field. (The papers were misplaced for several months after a cross-country move.) Since a regulatory agency was involved, a database for configuration of the equipment in the field in case of a recall was required. Of course, this included the software. We didn't take title until our field service visited each site and documented the software version numbers. We found multiple software versions in the field and since no test records were available, all undocumented equipment had to be pulled. Buying the company looked good on paper, but we ended up with a huge and costly configuration problem.

Lawyers and accountants do their own business audits when a company is being purchased. If software is a part of the company's main business or a major expense, it makes sense to look into the development. If you get called to do a buyout audit, make sure you go into every corner of the software. Read every piece of documentation and confirm that the product will work as shown. Also, read the corrective action database with all the open items. Review all the test plans and the results from these tests. Then make sure that the product is being developed according to the documentation. A generalization here: the owner would not be selling if everything were perfect. Proceed with that assumption— it's your job to find the places that are not perfect. There is no hard and fast rule about how long an audit should take; that will depend on the number and size of the projects.

Sometimes the software audit covers only one aspect of the development. Is the software lab equipment being maintained? This is an IT type of audit and should be done by the IT department. If the company has an IT department, there is no problem. If not, you may be asked to perform the audit. There might be areas outside your normal auditing comfort zone. Do some research and solicit areas of interest from the client. They usually have something that isn't resonating with them. Occasionally during the audit, it will become apparent that personnel are the problem. That is not an auditable domain; rather it's your opinion. As a fact finder, stick only to things you can document.

After a product has been released, a client may want an audit to find out the high-cost areas or where the process can be improved. Is there a weak area, and how can it be improved for the next project?

In Dr. W. Edwards Deming's "Some Obstacles," the seventh obstacle is listed as "Blaming the workforce for problems." He defines this:

"Workers are responsible for only 15 percent of the problems, the system for the other 85 percent. The system is the responsibility of management."[1]

Management isn't always aware of problems. It's not unusual for employees to sugarcoat reports, either from a desire to please or as a deliberate ruse. An outside person brings objectivity and through careful auditing will expose the shortcomings that require action. If the audit opens dialogue to fix the system, savings will go to the bottom line. The client should understand that if any management problems are found during the audit, they will be presented only to management with a private review to develop corrective actions.

3.1 PURPOSE

When you are called to audit, one of the first questions, you need to ask is "Why?" Though audits should be routinely performed to maintain a high standard of excellence, many times they are the result of a costly delay that has management starting to demand answers. But answers to what?

If you were told to "take the ship to a harbor with deep water and nice land around it" how would you know where to go? The statement is too broad. Which continent? Which ocean? Which country? Which city? You need a direction to focus on—it's the same with performing an audit.

For example the software did not ship and you have a frustrated customer. You have two main problems: why did you not hear about it before and what caused the delay?

To me, the bigger problem is the communication issue. Where did it break down? This was not a surprise to someone in the company. For whatever reason that information was not shared. The earlier that management knows about a delay, the easier it is to talk to the customer and adjust the delivery schedule. If the customer is told the day of delivery that there will be a delay, now he has a problem. There might be training classes scheduled, recent data (that might have taken a week to assemble) prepared to be entered into the system, or new hardware already

---

[1]"The Seven Deadly Diseases and Some Obstacles," from a Deming seminar sponsored by George Washington School of Engineering and Applied Science, San Diego, California, January 24–27, 1984.

installed. In other words, the customer could have a major investment in time, money and manpower that depends on the auditee's delivery. Customer satisfaction is key to repeat business and someone just dropped the ball.

There are many different problems that can come out of a software department. A missed delivery is just one. When problems arise and you have been called in by management to perform an audit, here are some questions to get you started:

- At whose request is the audit being done?

- Was the system delivered, but it didn't work?

  - Sometimes you might need to talk to a customer.

- Was the product delivered with missing functions?

  - Which functions and where were they dropped?

  - Was the function in the functional specification?

  - Was the function skipped or dropped during the design phase?

  - Was the specification for the programmer clear?

  - Was there too little time to complete the function?

- Is the final product too hard to use?

  - Was the customer involved with the user approach to run the programs?

- Did a product lock up or terminate during normal usage?

  - Restarting the system is very costly and frustrating.

- Were numbers on a report wrong or incomplete?

  - Was the product tested and proven to report the right data?

- Is the client going to be the end user?

  - Is this an internal system?

- Is the client an investor in the software development?

  - Did the project eat all the profits?

- Did the budget for next year come in with a large increase for development?

If management requested the audit, here are some additional areas they would want covered:

- Is the development compliant with regulations and standards?

- Are there any actual or potential software risks?

- Are there process risks?

- What areas are to be optimized?

- Are the system and processes effective?

- Can there be any improvement in the business performance?

- Are the resources being used to their fullest?

- Can the company improve the return on the software investment?

- Are there areas that are candidates for continuous improvement projects?

- Can inefficiencies in the systems and processes be identified?

- Is the system design adequate to achieve business objectives?

- Identify performance weaknesses and strengths

Most of the calls for audits are for projects that are not on schedule. You might end up showing the client that putting time into development risks could slow the development now but save time later. Also, there are many times that making some changes can pick up the pace to get the project back on track.

Cost can be an issue, but getting the project done right and on time are the biggest headaches. Don't get me wrong—money is money and cost does play a major part in business. Every company wants the product finished "at the lowest cost" possible. By this point, however, they just want it done and off their schedule.

Open communications is key. Sometimes you just need to sit with the clients and ask about areas of specific concern. What are their plans? Where do they see the greatest growth? Just make sure you listen more than talk.

When you are finished with the meeting(s), summarize what you think the client wants from the audit. If the client agrees, you are finished. If not, don't leave. Keep talking; you must have a purpose to be effective.

3.2 SCOPE

Scope is how wide and deep an area your client wants audited. Is it one project or all the projects within the department? Is it one function or more? Maybe it's one project audited from top to bottom.

Having learned from the client where their area of concern is, we have our focus. Perhaps what you've heard from the client is financial concerns. You would know to zero in on spending in all phases of development. You might start with a top-level audit, which could take two or three days. After coming across a problem, drill down to find more information. You might uncover a general problem, and the client with this information can take it to the root cause.

Gauging a time frame for an audit is difficult. There are many variables, ranging from the details given to you to the complexity of the product development to the cost projections to complete the audit. If the auditee sends you 10 documents ranging from 100 to 300 pages, the preparation would be a lot different than receiving four single pages of notes. Generally, the time frame is three to four days' preparation (based on the documents supplied), with an additional 4 to 10 days for the audit. How complex is the product? If the development is still in the design phase, you could be done in one week. At the other end of the spectrum, a full audit of a completed product might take a month from start of preparation to closing report. This is because the scope of the desired information would be wide, including a "lesson learned" section of great benefit to the client before starting the next project. Management might be interested in restructuring the software team, or the development process, thereby increasing cost savings and speeding up time to market.

3.3 MANAGEMENT'S PART IN AN AUDIT

This audit will go only as far as management allows it to go. If management does not announce the pending audit and tell employees that they are to give full cooperation to the auditors, the chances of a useful audit start to dissolve. Management cannot sit in the background and just watch. They must show support.

They need to talk up the audit and show up at the opening meeting. They should say a few words so employees know that management wants the audit results. If employees know that management will be studying and reviewing the results, they will get the message that they cannot blow off the audit. The higher the level of management in attendance at the meeting, the better. You bring the objectivity, but you can't produce a fair and accurate audit if you don't have full disclosure. You've probably heard the term "garbage in, garbage out" as it applies to data entry—it's also applicable here. Without facts, you get a manufactured fairy tale, not an accurate representation of status.

NOTE: In a buyout or merger, you will need the full support from the buying and selling managements to get a better audit. But remember, in cases like this people will try their best to hide problems from the new management to keep their jobs. If you know this going in, you are ahead of the game.

3.4 PREPARING FOR THE AUDIT

Before you move on to this section you need to talk to the client about a proprietary or confidentiality agreement. Companies want to know that what you are seeing and hearing is not shared with or repeated to anyone else. Take care of this before you request any documents.

You now know the purpose and scope of the audit, but you're still not ready to roll up your sleeves and begin. You need to know what is going on in development by requesting the project's documentation So you do not waste their time or yours, familiarizing yourself with their development style might shed light on potential problem areas. If the auditee has been in development for a length of time, they might have most of the documents on the following list. But if the software department is not that mature, ask for all and hope you get something. A good idea is to give them a list of the documents you will want to see.

Here is a list to request:

Quality Documents

1. Company quality manual

2. Company's vision and mission statements

3. Software development plan including SDLC

4. Configuration control plan

5. Corrective action plan

6. Software quality plan

7. Program plan and program quality plan

8. Unit testing plan

9. Functional test plan

10. Integration test plan

11. Acceptance test plan

Development Documents

12. Organizational chart

13. Both software and program risk registers or reports

14. List of standards the company uses

15. All development processes and procedures

16. All development work instructions

17. Sales order or statement of work

18. Software/project schedule

19. Functional specifications

20. Design specifications

21. Software specifications

22. Peer review documents

23. Copies of change requests (only one or two requests)

24. Copies of bug reports (only one or two)

25. Copies of minutes from customer reviews

If the client is also the auditee, it is easy to get the documents. If the client is a third party such as a customer or even upper management, request the documents with the announcement of the audit. Make sure you give yourself enough time to read all the documents. If you receive all the documents listed above, you have a better chance of covering the whole project.

The document review can take as much time as the audit itself. Software audits are different from other audits. The principals of accounting do not change between clients; only the background data is different. In software you need to understand what they are doing and how they are doing it. You could end up with hundreds of pages to read and digest before the audit begins.

The fewer documents you receive, the more time you will spend at the auditee site doing the audit. If you are performing an audit on the whole software development department, it could take additional time on site to get a better feel of the software project. Departments or projects combining schedules and resource plans are an additional complication.

There is a breakdown of the documents you receive in Chapter 14, Review Software Documents. The more you understand of the development, the more your audit will provide the tools for the auditee to improve their system.

4

Opening Meeting

When I do a standard opening meeting, I ask that both management and auditees attend. Depending on the size and scope of the audit, the requirements and protocol I follow might change. I will ask for a brief tour either before or right after the opening meeting. Then I schedule 30 minutes to an hour for overview from the product team. Both the tour and review will be covered in more detail later in this chapter.

The opening meeting is the start of the official audit. Many people in the company will not even know there is an audit scheduled until the meeting is announced. I explain before the meeting that I will need a work space and an escort(s) during the audit. Any proprietary issues and confidentiality agreements should have been taken care of before you received the documentation for preparation reviews. Depending on your company and your client, there might need to be a transfer of security clearances before the audit.

4.1 THE MEETING

The opening meeting, sometimes called the "entrance meeting," should have a simple agenda. Upon entering the meeting room, either the audit team or the auditee should start the introductions and get all the hand shaking finished. Do not be afraid to ask for a person's title or how they fit into the department. As the attendees settle down, tell them all about the sign-in sheet being passed around. It is part of the documentation—a quality record of the meeting.

Here is a usual agenda:

Opening Meeting

- Introductions.

- Present the purpose and scope of the audit.

- Review the findings of any previous audits.

- Explain that this is a quality audit and what a quality audit is.

- Explain how the audit will work.

- Explain the questions.

- Point out the escorts and management contacts.

- Explain the daily meetings.

- Ask for questions.

4.1.1 Introductions

During the introduction make sure you thank your host. Introduce yourself with your credentials. Try to set the mood of the meeting as relaxed to dispel any apprehension. Introduce the rest of your team (if there is a team) and give their credentials. Explain where each auditor will be working. Have someone keep the minutes of the meeting and make sure you get a copy of the minutes and attendance for your records.

4.1.2 Present the Purpose and Scope of the Audit

The client who has contracted for the audit has laid out the purpose and scope of the audit. The lead auditor will now have to explain the purpose and the scope.

The purpose can be a very generic statement such as, "Audit the configuration management used on the project or auditing the test procedures for the product."

The purpose of this audit is to understand how the software development is performed. The auditor will be looking at the steps taken to develop the product. The auditor will look at the controls and how they are being followed. As a result of the audit, the company will have the information necessary for action. It is up to management. List the documents that have been reviewed.

4.1.3 Review Previous Audits

If you have conducted audits before at this auditee, you might want to say a *few* words about it. Don't open any old wounds; people will remember on their own. Keep it short and light.

4.1.4 Explain the Quality Audit

Explain what a quality audit really covers. Let's look at a manufacturing example to illustrate the audit path. If we were looking at a toaster, the auditor would look at the final product to make sure that all the parts go together and that the toaster works. If the production line had not yet built the first unit, the auditor would go to the production line and make sure that each piece going into the toaster was made correctly and that the line was ready to begin.

Likewise, if the software product was complete, the auditor would look at the final product and see if it is made to specifications in the original design. If the software is in the development cycle, the auditor would review the development process to ascertain that the team is in compliance with the requirements.

The next part of a quality audit is the process part. In this area, our toaster would be looked at during the making of the parts to see that they are made the same each time. Think of the assembly line and how a sequence of actions delivers a final product. In software the order is: module designed, coded, unit tested, and sent to system testing.

The next section is the quality section. Was the wiring of the toaster done to the UL standard? It is the same way with software. Has the code been written to a standard? Whether it's a toaster or software, both are produced following a detailed sequence of steps that adhere to a standard.

4.1.5 Explain How the Audit Will Work

The audit started with an offsite review of documents sent to the audit team. These documents were reviewed for content and an understanding of the product being developed.

The plan for the audit is to have an informal overview of the product for 15 to 30 minutes with the questions that came up during the document review. These questions could be either direct questions or clarifications.

At this point, I will usually give a quick overview of the interview questions and introduce the escorts. They will be my link to escort interviewees and bring me additional documentation.

4.1.6 Daily Meetings

Daily meetings are held by the audit team to coordinate their findings and also to keep the client informed. In addition, the audit team might meet to prioritize or rearrange assignments to help the flow of the audit. They might review any findings to see if the same finding occurred in other areas. They could start gathering data for the exit meeting.

In the morning, there might be a 5- to 10-minute meeting for schedule or plan changes. The auditor might have found something in a document that the auditor would like to have clarified, or there might be a new direction to be pursued.

4.1.7 Questions and Answers

Give the auditee's employees a chance to ask questions. You want to promote this as a joint effort. They need to know you are willing to work with them. You will not get to the truth if there is any misunderstanding on either side.

4.2 AN ESCORT

The escort should know his way around the development area and know what people are working on for quick responses to questions that come up. The escort should be able to point out proprietary areas that the auditor enters. The escort also should understand safety and regulatory requirements that the auditor could come in contact with during the audit.

The escort should introduce the auditor to the employees before interviews. Managers are not good candidates to be escorts, because it's a waste of their time and employees get nervous when they're around. During interviews, the escort can leave to do other things or get the next person to interview. If the auditor needs clarification of information, the escort should be able to answer the questions. Findings are always reported to the escort. The escort should keep management up to date on the progress of the audit.

The escort is not accompanying you so that he may argue each finding. If this is the case, contact management and ask for another escort. If the escort is a quality person, he will understand what you are doing and want to learn about the findings.

4.3 WORK SPACE

The auditee needs to know that the auditor needs a "home base," a quiet place for interviews. This workspace will be used to gather working papers and review documents when necessary, so it should be dedicated for the length of the audit. Do not use the company's executive conference room; that is too intimidating for an employee. Use a team room, empty office, or a conference room that everyone has used often.

4.4 A BRIEF TOUR

The auditor needs to see where the development is taking place. This includes the desk area and the software labs. The work environment might give a hint of how they think and what they value. You are trying to get a feel for the place. Is it neat, or is there stuff all over the place? The more things lying around, the deeper you need to explore. If the desks are messy, make sure there are version controls in place. Any accessibility limitations placed on the audit team should be identified during the tour.

In the labs, ask about what functions are performed at a station. Watch for build stations (where the source becomes machine language). If there is more than one, do they both produce the same executable code? Look for testing stations; are there stations dedicated for testing? Ask about test equipment and how it works. Is there a mock-up of the system being developed? Can they change operating systems, or are there different machines with different operating systems?

In the office area, ask about how many people can do a build of the software on their systems. Who does the final build? What kind of network are the computers connected to and where are the development servers? Ask where the developer(s), tester(s), and support people sit.

This is all background data that you can use later to confirm what you are told. For example: you ask about testers and are told there are three, but during the tour the guide said the company doesn't have testers. Now, you have to dig deep to see what they are doing. They might be hiring three testers or transferring them from another project. How much start-up time will they need in order to be productive? Is this included in the schedule?

4.5 MEETING THE PEOPLE

During the tour, ask questions about the people you see working:

manager		How many people are on the project?
		How many people are in each function?
everyone		What do you do?
everyone		How long have you been working on this job?
everyone		How many people have requested or put in for transfers to other groups or team jobs?

You are looking for turnover. You are looking for people leaving without giving notice. You are not judging anyone; you are only raising the question of the turnover. Do not count people who have received promotions. I have seen half a team leave within seven months without anyone questioning the cause. It could be filtered from reports to management because of the format of the report. I understand that this is really a human resources problem, but you are here to find out about a problem in development—a constantly changing cast of characters will alter the flow and outcome.

Another area of personnel you might want to watch for is key people being shifted from crisis to crisis. Try to build some history here. Do people need training? Do they have the proper skill set? Is the crisis real? Is information being shared? Does the manager move workers from crisis to crisis, or is it informal within the group? Here are questions to ask:

		Are there too many fires?
		Is the same troubleshooter putting all the fires out?
		List the last three months' crises and who fixed them.
		Does the team have one person who is the information center and is not the manager?
		Does the team share information?
		What is the general mood of the team?

An unhappy workplace will affect the outcome.

4.6 INFORMAL OVERVIEW PRESENTATION

Now that you've had your opening meeting, been assigned a work space, and had a brief tour, you might find this optional step useful. You can read all of the documentation about a project, but sometimes you just need an overview to help you put the pieces together. This is your call. Have a status review presented to you or attend a management status review to get a look at what they are telling managers. It also gives you a feel of whether they know what they are doing. There should be a couple of overheads, PowerPoint slides, or handouts to help explain the system. Any problems or software risks should be shown. They should have them already created to present to their customers. At the end of that meeting is a good time to ask general questions or special questions about the documents.

Useful questions to ask:

		Do you feel this presentation has been done before?
		Are people interrupting one another to fill in gaps?
		Is the data presented smoothly?
		Is anyone surprised by facts or claims?
		Is anyone rolling their eyes during the presentation?

NOTE: Body language is often your best clue.

Do not question any of the above situations during this meeting. Wait until you have the person alone and then question what was happening.

The next step will be interviews with people who work in different areas in development. These people will be managers, designers, programmers, testers, configuration, and quality people. We might even throw in a purchasing agent. During the interviews, they might be asked to supply documents that they referenced during the interview. Those might include minutes, logs, procedures, test scripts, or other documents that might help the auditor. These documents become working papers to help get the clearest picture of the software development process.

During the preparation time for the audit, group the questions by job titles. During the opening meeting or directly after, just fill in the name of the person with the title into the schedule. This gives you an interview schedule for the auditee and escort to follow. You can make changes as you go if someone is not available. Try to get the escort to confirm interviews one or two meetings ahead on the schedule.

4.7 EXPLAIN THE QUESTIONS

The questions asked during the interviews are to gain better insight into the development process. The employee might be talking to someone else and find out that the auditor asked the same question of that person. It is not that the auditor forgot the answer; it is to make sure everyone uses the same framework. Sometimes different people answer the same question with extra details that help the auditor draw a conclusion. If employees do not understand the question, they should ask for more information. This is their workplace and the auditor is an outsider who does not understand the ways things are done.

During the interviews something might surface—for example, that building of software modules is not performed the same way every time. This would be a finding. The finding could be a risk area or not a recommended practice. The interviewee and the escort will be shown the problem and it will be explained. A finding could be a nonconformity or noncompliance to a standard the company is using. There could be an improvement point or cost savings finding made for the company's review in the final report.

The answers will be recorded to be analyzed later with other answers, so just because the auditor is writing does not mean something is wrong. If the employee believes that the auditor does not understand the answer, the auditor will be open to discussion. There will be no "Joe said" in the final report. The names are recorded for the auditor's records only.

If an employee is asked to show an auditor some function, it is for a better understanding. Of course, it might lead to more questions.

The findings will be classified categories and rated on a scale of critical to low. There might be a suggested timeframe for action.

5

Conducting the Audit

How do people picture an auditor? Someone told me they picture a man who rubs his hands together and snickers with glee when he identifies a finding. It's not a pretty image. Auditors are generally perceived as intruders or trouble makers. On the contrary, our goal as auditor is to be an objective reviewer and help the auditee deliver a final product that will do their business proud.

If you are using this book as a guide and have never done an audit before, you might be wondering, "How do I find out the information I need to answer all these questions?" This chapter addresses this.

Attitude-wise, the auditee will follow your lead. If you joke around when asking the questions, the auditee will not take the audit seriously. If you walk in with a face cast in stone, you will make people defensive or wary and it is not going to be a very good audit. You want to be friendly and personable, and convey an attitude of confidence that together good work is in progress.

Upon receipt of documents sent to you for review, you should begin formulating ideas on how you want to approach the audit. Develop a rough flowchart of what areas you want to audit, and then build your checklist. If you are performing a formal audit, dates for the audit should be scheduled and you should send the auditee a copy of your checklist.

Although management sent you to audit software development and may have highlighted perceived problems, you still need to review the software documents and zero in on the areas that stand out. If you don't understand what is being developed, management can bury you in details that have nothing to do with the problems. They will test you on your knowledge of their system. If you stand there like a deer in the headlights, you will find out very little about the problem and lose your credibility. When you ask a pointed question about the system, showing you understand it, they will give you direct answers and less smoke and mirrors.

A sample checklist and a finding form is at the end of this chapter.

5.1 ROLES OF THE AUDITORS

When you are assigned to perform the audit, you will be doing it either alone or as part of a team. When you work as part of a team, you will need to know the responsibility of each member.

5.1.1 Lead Auditor

When an auditor has been told that they are going to be lead auditor on an audit, their work begins right away. The lead auditor must meet with the client, audit manager, or management to define the objectives. An initial plan must be mapped out. The lead auditor must contact the auditee to find out what documents are available and to get copies. He also must send out the checklist, if that is necessary.

The lead auditor should meet with the auditing team to check the availability of the team and the specialties of the members. He should give a broad description of the auditee and the project being developed.

When the software documents arrive, the lead should do a preliminary review to develop the plan. The documents that will be common for all members and those that are special for each team member's area of the audit should be distributed. The team should meet again to discuss the project before starting the audit.

The leader should send out the audit notice with the audit plan and make arrangements with the auditee for conference and interview rooms. Additionally, he should explain the escort duties so one or more can be provided. The audit team's leader will handle the communications with the client and auditee management or representative.

The team manager's normal responsibilities include chairing the opening meeting, directing the team, keeping the audit moving, chairing the (daily) process meetings, chairing the closing meeting, writing the audit report, mitigating conflicts, and keeping the auditee informed of findings. After the report has been sent, copies need to be filed and stored.

5.1.2 Auditor

In the event this is a small audit, then the auditor assumes the role and responsibilities of the lead. To start the process of auditing, the auditor needs to understand the purpose and scope of the audit. If the audit is to a standard, the auditor must be familiar with it. If the audit is part of an investigation of development problems, the auditor needs to know what prompted the audit.

The lead auditor should supply a list of each section of the development and specify what he/she wants covered by this auditor. The auditor will need to develop a checklist using the software documents that were reviewed.

During the audit, the auditor will use the checklist, writing the responses and collecting evidence to verify conformance or nonconformance. During the team meetings at the end of the day, the auditor should report any nonconformance findings. Any conflicts or audit timing problems should be discussed with the lead.

Of course, the auditor should attend all meetings such as opening, daily, and closing meetings. The auditor's report becomes part of the closing meeting. After the site visit is complete, the auditor's input to the formal report is important.

Sometimes the auditor is assigned the task of following up on corrections. The due dates must be observed and reminders sent to the person responsible. The auditor verifies the corrections and report the results.

5.2 THE AUDIT

Now you are going to begin the audit. How you handle this is how the people will respond to you. A skilled auditor can put people at ease and encourage them to be cooperative. Every system is different and you will not understand them all. There are systems out there that break every rule to do a special job. Stick to the basics, and do not judge the design. You are not questioning the design, and do not get into a conflict over it.

Spend a few minutes before each interview to put your interviewee at ease. Understanding what this person's job is and his level within the job will help you frame the questions. Whenever you are talking to someone, give them your undivided attention. It just might be that the person has what you are seeking. Do not assume you know the answer from someone else you have interviewed. Tell the interviewee the purpose of the interview. Also tell them that you will be taking notes and it does not mean something is wrong. Tell the interviewee that with all the people you end up talking to, it can get very confusing without notes. If you need to write long answers, tell them that they just explained something you did not understand and to please be patient while you quickly write it down. Sometimes you can write a quick note and add details between interviews. One last point: Write at a normal pace. If you write at a panicky pace, they will worry. Record the person's name and title for your use only. Let the interviewee know that you will not connect an answer to any person. It can be very interesting when you get different answers to the same question. It's up to you to figure out if this is a flexible point or the problem. It will certainly inspire a new set of questions in your quest to zero in.

When you ask someone about how they do something, and they tell you there is a process, procedure, or work instruction. Ask to see it. When you get it, *read it.* It may differ from the documents you read prior to starting the audit.

At the end of the interview, tell the interviewee your preliminary conclusions. If you have a finding, explain it and let them add information that might clear the finding. If the person knows their job and there is no finding, say so. If the person is doing an excellent job, say, "You are doing an excellent job." My rule is to find something positive to say before a negative. Never debate a finding.

5.3 WORK SHEET/CHECKLIST

You will need a checklist to perform an audit. A checklist is a document that lays out the questions you are going to ask. We want to ask open-ended questions and to avoid yes-no answers. Example: Do you drive a car? (yes/no answer). What kind of car do you drive? (open-ended). You want the person to talk freely and expand the answer. The checklist keeps the audit on track. If something outside the checklist comes to your attention, you can follow the trail. The checklist will get you back on the scheduled questions.

The auditing team will create the checklist before the opening meeting. The checklist should be sent to the auditee before the audit. This will give the auditee time to gather answers and documentation for the questions. In a perfect world the checklist will help the auditee know what is coming and where the auditor will be looking. It also shows the auditee if there are things missing in their development. If the development group starts to put together information and fill some gaps, the audit is already helping.

I use a program that I developed as my checklist because I track many more pieces of information. I started by using spreadsheets and tables in a word processing program. If you find yourself doing lots of audits, develop a system that works for you in your particular audit environment.

During the questioning, suppose that the answer references a document. What do you do? First, write the document name (number) in the comment area. Ask for a copy. If the document is available, mark the question number on the cover. If the document is not available and someone is getting it, write the person's name next to the document's name. This is your reminder of who to haunt until the paperwork is provided.

If the documents are confidential, get a copy of the cover page and write the page number or section number on your copy. This becomes part of your working pages (or evidence). If the answer is different than the specifications or any other document, it is a finding. Put a check or "X" with a circle around it in the question column and tell the escort. When you have a finding, fill out the finding form described later in this chapter. Don't argue with the escort; just let him/her know you have a finding. If they can come up with evidence to show you are wrong, look at it and add it to the documentation.

Figure 5.1 shows a checklist created in Microsoft Excel (you can use any spreadsheet program). If you are using a spreadsheet program, you might want to add a findings column. Then you can use the power of the spreadsheet to sort out the findings.

Checklist			
Date:			
Company Name:			
Contact Name:			
Who	**#**	**Questions**	**Response/Comments**
manager	1	Are all the programmers using the same operating system?	
everyone	2	What operating system is on your PC?	
manager	3	Do all the programmers have the same compiler?	
everyone	4	What compilers do you use?	
manager	5	What version of the libraries do the programs use?	
everyone	6	What libraries do you use?	
manager/ programmer	7	What is the revision or version number of the library?	
manager	8	Who builds the software?	
	9		
	10		
	11		
	12		

Figure 5.1   Checklist form.

The headings on the checklist are what I used. You can change it to suit your type of audit or company standards. If you use a table in a word processing program, you lose the power of sorting, but it is still useful. You need to work with the tools that are available to you.

5.4 FINDINGS FORM

Figure 5.2 is the form I use to record findings. If on the checklist you marked that there is a finding, the findings form is where you record the details. Do you need to use this form? No, but it gives you more room to write up the details and starts the corrective action.

Never put the name of the person(s) on a findings form. The old audits put blame on the individual. There are many auditors out there still doing this. The current practice is to attribute the finding to the real problem: the process. In the

Findings Form	
Auditee Name	**Date**
Project Name	**Question Number**
Findings/Observation	
Objective Evidence	
Immediate Action	
	Name Date
Temporary Actions	
	Name Date
Permanent Actions	
	Name Date

For each change, please send a copy to: Auditor, 123 Any Way St.

Figure 5.2   Findings information sheet.

past, people were sometimes fired because their name was listed with a problem. Management's thought was, "Person gone, problem gone." Unfortunately, the process stayed the same and the results were the same.

Fill in the heading section before the opening meeting so you need only to fill in question number and finding/observation (F/O) when performing the actual audit.

Header section of form:

- **Auditee name**—Who you are auditing (company name).

- **Date**

- **Project name**

- **Question Number**—This comes from the checklist so you can go back and look for more details.

You might want to add more to the headings, such as:

- Your name

- Audit number

- Client name

- Time

- Finding number

The body of the form is:

- **Findings/Observation**—What you found and where you found it.

- **Objective Evidence**—What you did to confirm this finding or what document this finding does not match. Write down what was said by someone other than the original interviewee that concurs with the findings (no names)

- **Immediate Action**—What is the auditee doing right away to avoid the problem until it is permanently fixed?

- **Temporary Action**—What is being done until the root cause is found and the problems fixed?

- **Permanent Action**—The root cause fix.

All three actions are discussed in Chapter 7, "Audit Follow-up and Closure."

In each of the actions at the bottom, there is a place for a name and date. These are for the person who implemented the fix at the action level. On the bottom of the page is the statement "For each change, please send a copy to:" that urges the auditee to notify you of any work done on the problem so you can track it.

6

Meetings and Final Report

You have ended your research part of the audit and the last interview. You now take your notes, checklists, and working papers and review what you have done. By now you have opinions on the audit. You know where some of the findings are and where some of the questionable information is. You probably have snippets of information, bits and pieces that by themselves mean very little. These may become relevant during the caucus meetings—if not to your part of the audit, then probably to someone else's section.

The next three parts of the audit are:

- Caucus meeting

- Exiting or closing meeting

- Final report

6.1 CAUCUS MEETING

The caucus is the meeting for only the auditors. It is like the jurors in a trial—you get to go over the evidence that each person brings to the table. First, you get the overall feeling from each person. The lead auditor is more of a facilitator, making sure everyone can speak freely. This is brainstorming at its best. As the team talks about the overview of the audit, a hot spot will begin to surface. Then the team starts to zero in on the findings and analyze the data. Does the finding support the general feeling? If a new finding comes together because of facts from different auditors, I let the management representative know after the caucus what was found, and why it is a finding. I don't like to have surprises in the exiting meeting.

Determine whether there are any areas that are outstanding in their approach, process, or procedures. There is usually some part of the development that is above the rest. Make sure that the development team gets the credit for doing an excellent job in that area.

As the audit team comes to a conclusion about the causes and patterns they have seen, they will be able to place the findings into a priorities list. Finally, the exiting report is put together. All findings must be in the exiting report; any that are not presented at the exiting meeting cannot be in the final report.

Review the list of findings to make sure that the findings have been confirmed or have evidence. Do not accept one instance to create a finding; examine all the data and if the team needs more information, have someone leave the meeting and go confirm the evidence. Use the following five types of evidence:

- Documents and records—self explanatory

- Interviews—written checklist with statement showing the finding

- Physical—screen print-outs or equipment configurations

- Observations—something noted by the audit that may become a finding

- Patterns—something out of the normal process that is different than the pattern

You might have to do some extra explaining with patterns. Perhaps show graphs or data that support the problem.

The actual report lists the findings in priority order. I like to point out where the finding is a risk and how high the risk is to the project. The rating of the risks is left to the final report after we've had more time to review the facts. Any additional information, such as cost savings and areas of improvement, can be added so that the auditee has a starting point.

6.2 CLOSING (EXITING) MEETING

The closing meeting usually takes about an hour. Minutes will be taken, as this process is all part of the final report. Take the attendance at the beginning of the meeting. Make introductions, so everyone knows who is at the meeting. Thank your host for allowing your team to perform the audit.

Give a general overview of the team's opinion about the audit. If it is really bad news, you might want to wait until you have explained your findings. By then, people will be drawing their own conclusions and it won't be such a shot out of left field. Explain what areas were audited and thank the people from these areas for their cooperation.

Try to use PowerPoint or something similar so that the people can see the words and the evidence. You do not need to hand out your notes in their rough form. Your review starts with the highest-priority finding. Explain the finding and how you came across it. It is your decision whether you want to have a discussion about the findings. If you discuss a finding, make sure most people understand the finding before moving on. An agreement could be made that you are getting together after the meeting to review new evidence.

You set the tone of the meeting. Keep your voice interesting, not monotone. Stay factual, but relaxed and pleasant, and your findings will be more readily accepted.

Again thank everyone before you close the meeting. Stay around for the informal discussions to answer questions. Sometimes management will ask for a quick meeting to go over things that could be done to correct the problems. If part of the scope of the audit is to write up corrective action requests, explain that you will include them in your final report—but you can do a short oral summary.

If there is a major difference of opinion about a finding, arrange for proof to be sent to you or take the proof before you leave. Then review the finding as soon as possible while the audit is fresh in your mind. The most time I would allow for the proof to arrive at my office is one week. You need to be able to write up your final report and deliver it within the agreed upon period of time.

6.3 FINAL REPORT

Most audit books suggest that the final report be sent or delivered within 30 days. No auditor I know lets the final report go that far. I like to send or deliver the report within two weeks, and I average about eight business days. The sooner the auditee and client have the report, the faster the project can get on track.

This is what should be included in your final report:

- Executive summary

- Audit objective

- Purpose and scope

- Identification of the client

- Identification of the auditee (department, project) and company

- Identification of the audit team leader and members

- A statement of the confidentiality agreement

- List of documents reviewed during preparation for the audit

- Preparation dates

- List of the standards (ISO, IEEE, and so on) used for the audit

- The audit dates and on-site audit location

- Risk elements

- Description of areas with findings/nonconformities

  - Specific requirements

  - Number of findings

  - Opportunities for improvement

  - References to corrective action requests

- Audit conclusions

- Detailed findings with evidence

- Recommendations for improvement

- Distribution list for the report

If I audit a procedure or section and have no findings, I will still show the questions with the answers. For example, if an audit reports that the software configuration area has been audited and there are no findings, the client needs to know what was looked at and to understand that all aspects of the software configuration have been looked into and found in good shape. False or incomplete information can be worse than no information at all.

I take a different approach with my final report. The extra items I include are aimed at the software management. This information will help them make better decisions for the project. These variations are necessary because of the complex development process. The following description will help to explain the need for the changes.

6.3.1 Executive Summary

The executive summary is three or four paragraphs that give an overview of the audit. There is a summary of the statistics, such as:

- Total number of each level of findings

- Total number of each level of risk to the project

- Number of cost saving findings

- Number of improvements and time to implement

- Number of risks found

The team will be recognized as competent and unbiased if the summary presents a professional, honest, and straightforward picture.

6.3.2 Identify Documents Reviewed

The client needs to know what information the auditor saw before the audit. A list of requirement or specification documents includes the revision number with a paragraph giving an audit overview and/or any major findings found. If a request for a complete review of the document was made by the client, the list of all findings will be included. If you had a meeting to discuss the document findings, you can leave out the paragraph.

The list will include the auditee's policies, quality manuals, work schedules, and special software procedures. Review time will be needed if a lesser-known standard is used for special industries.

6.3.3 Preparation Dates

Dates on which the auditee supplied documents are listed.

6.3.4 Specify the Standards

Like every other audit, these documents will be used for nonconformities. If no standard is used, this section explains the criteria on which the findings are based.

6.3.5 Software Risk Analysis

This section highlights all the risk factors that were found. These could include missing documents such as test plan and design specifications. This section could include out-of-phase findings.

I have developed a software risk analysis that is included in the report. This is an area that is "competition sensitive."

6.3.6 Description of Areas

As this book explains, there are many areas to be checked in a software development project. List all the areas you audited, including areas that have no findings. This will relieve the worry that an area was not audited at all.

The maturity of R&D will affect your report. The older the system, the more systemic findings you will come across. If the company is new to software development, you will find many open areas where they are skipping good practices. You may report any conclusion based on the evidence, your judgment, or your understanding of the auditee's situation.

Other information would include a summary of the findings found with the findings number to reference the details at the end of the report. Point out opportunities for improvement and list references to the corrective action requests detailed at the end of the report. You may also report opportunities for improvement, best practices, and areas where stronger procedures are needed.

6.4 WRITING THE REPORT

"The audit report should provide a complete, accurate, concise, and clear record of the audit." This is from ISO 19011, clause 6.6.1. You should also include traceability in your report. Write the report as if someone who had nothing to do with the audit is reading it. You want to give them the best information so that they can make the best decision.

Unlike the exit meeting report, you have time to go over the facts and report them in greater detail. Present the data as if you are addressing a management board. Keep it direct and as simple as possible. Use the terminology that makes auditee management comfortable. Avoid acronyms and give definitions for greater clarity. Keep the tone of the report courteous and professional, and based on confirmed data and without personal prejudice. Always remember your job is to be an objective resource for the client.

To make your points, prepare a section to show the software risks that the findings would cause if no action is taken, including customer satisfaction, costs, savings, and development time. Be conservative in your statements. If two programmers tell you that a tester could save them 10 to 15 hours a week, use only the lower number of 10 in your report. If managers ask the programmers what they think it could save them, your statement will be accepted at face value. Let the management do the math; they will get the point. Use a graph so facts are easier to visualize.

Stick to one format for your reports. Over time you can refine it to your needs. After you have completed a few reports, you will start thinking about the writing during the audit itself.

As in the exit report, make sure you highlight processes, procedures, or functions that are doing a good job. Management should already be aware of strengths, but by pointing them out you validate their choice of you as their auditor and you lend credibility to negative findings.

Make sure that the audit team leader/manager signs and dates the report. If you are going to send out the report via e-mail, put the report in PDF format so that there is less chance of tampering. After the client has reviewed the report and approves it, distribute copies to everyone on the list at the same time. You will have a lot fewer headaches about people getting them late. In addition to the e-mail, send a hard copy for the client's files.

6.5 DETAIL FINDING PAGES

These are the supporting pages for the report. Put one finding on each page and give as many details as possible. If there are nonconformities to a company standard, you do not need a long description of the finding.

But if there are no standards and you are using good practices for your finding, you will need a more in-depth explanation. Here is an example:

Finding: There is no configuration control on source code.

Reason for Finding: During the interviews, 6 out of 10 programmers were not using a controlled document software package.

- *Your programmers must know they are working on the latest version.* Programmers usually have more than one copy of source on their PC. It wastes money to update the wrong version or working version.

- *Configuration control keeps copies of old versions.* If a problem develops in the field and you don't know when it started, you can go back through old versions and find a starting point for your investigation.

- *Control branches of your software.* Different customers require changes only for their application. Update each branch when new features are added or a problem has been found.

- *If a problem develops, you know who is using that version.* You must know where each revision of your software is installed. If a problem is found you might need to issue a recall or an update.

- *Control software is usually backed up weekly.* Programmers tend not to back up their PC. When a program source is in configuration control, it automatically does a back-up.

This was a simple example to illustrate how to write a detail findings page. For your audit report, you will have to explain the major reason the finding was found. Include all your findings, because you are trying to persuade someone to work on the problem. Yes, you just became a salesperson, too. Show management there is good reason to fix the problem, and they will follow through with the corrective actions.

You might end up noting a finding was a symptom. Sometimes there are little problems that seem to be connected and you can't put your finger on the problem. You will not know the reasons for the problem. The auditee needs to do a root cause analysis on the problem to close it out. Don't try to debug code on the fly; let the programmer find the root cause. The more information you can give the auditee, the better the chances that the cause will be found.

6.6 PRESENTING THE REPORT

It is not unusual to be asked to return to the client to explain your report. Software is not understood by everyone. Make your presentation clear and concise. Use examples and charts to make your point. Leave the floor open for questions at any time. If asked to explain a point for a second time, do not repeat the same explanation. Try another angle to define the terms or simplify it.

6.7 CORRECTIVE ACTION REQUESTS

The corrective action request is a form requesting that the finding be fixed. This creates a record that can be tracked. The form contains:

- Date

- Name of the auditee

- Date(s) of audit

- Finding's identification number and audit number

- The finding

- Evidence

Filled in by auditee:

- Short-term action

- Root cause statement

- Long-term corrective action

- Who is responsible for the resolution and tracking of the finding

- Time frame for both the short-term action and long-term resolution

Don't be tempted to suggest a corrective action. Usually there is a lot more behind a problem than an auditor will know, so let the auditee's personnel figure out what needs to be done. That way they own the solution and they will most likely stick to it. If you recommend a fix, how are you going to audit that fix next time? You would be writing a finding on your own suggestion and there goes your objectivity. Answering all questions about the finding is the best help you can give.

It is an accepted practice that in your auditor role you can send out reminders for upcoming corrective action completion dates. Copy management with this correspondence and maintain your file until the customer has a permanent solution and closure has been achieved.

7

Audit Follow-up and Closure

Generally, not all clients require the auditor to do follow up. I've seen cases with a high number of findings where the decision is made to dump the project rather than take corrective action. Someone has paid a lot of money for an audit (internal, as well as external) because they believe in the product but want to be sure they are moving in the right direction. Do resources need to be moved around, and what does the department need to continue doing?

Another option is do nothing, to continue developing the same exact way. They know the risks and accept them.

No law says that the findings from an auditor must be completed. Perhaps the fixes cannot be implemented because of cost. It is management's choice on what happens and what action they take.

An unpleasant reality is that sometimes findings will be marked as corrected but development will continue exactly as before the audit. Unfortunately management often thinks the audit has failed, when it's employee non-compliance that is the problem. When that type of subterfuge is underway, management won't notice until missed schedules, missed deliveries, incomplete work, and customer dissatisfaction start to appear.

> There are other reasons that audit findings are falsely marked as completed. Sometimes it's the desire to get management out of the department so work can be re-started with the intent to fix it later. Other times a partial fix is recorded as complete. Either way, when you are called back to audit or the documentation fails to show up, the truth comes out.

Now that you have given the final report and a list of the findings, the client needs to make the next step.

Depending on your contract, part of the audit might be developing a corrective actions sheet for each finding. In many cases, the auditee will take over after receipt of the report. These sheets are more detailed than the findings in the final report. No matter who writes up the corrective actions sheets, only the auditee can fix the problems.

The auditee must define the problem and propose a solution. If you've been retained to follow this audit through to action completed, then you might be asked to review the definition and proposed solutions for the findings. After reviewing the corrective action sheet, the auditor can state either that the corrective action is not going to correct the problem or that not enough research has been done on the root cause.

The client needs to decide who will track the findings. It can be done with an internal database and someone monitoring the results. This will work if management reviews the changes.

No matter who writes the corrective action or tracks the findings, there are steps that should be taken. First, define the problem in the best way possible. The more details that are included, the better the solution. The company should look at the solution to determine a corrective action time frame. Is there an action to be taken immediately, such as stopping delivery, or something more complex that will take six months to put into the system? The auditee needs to decide if intermediate steps are required until the final solution is in place.

Here is an example. The finding is that there is no bug tracking system. It might take a few weeks to research programs to do the tracking and get a purchase order. The problem can be addressed immediately by making up a paper form to be used when bugs are detected. The bug reports will be put in a book in the manager's office for reference, and a copy will be forwarded to the programmer. Developing a procedure for the paper copies will make it a temporary fix. This temporary fix will work until the automated bug tracker is installed and all the old bug sheets are added to the database. Updating the database would make the program the permanent fix, and the paper system would go away.

The Corrective Action Request form needs a section to be for proposed action. The plan should show the time frame of the fix step by step. The approximate time of completion will give you a time when an on-site mini-audit could be performed. Even if the action is no action, there should be a write-up. Keep this in your quality records.

There are three types of proactive changes to take: immediate, temporary, and permanent.

7.1 IMMEDIATE ACTIONS

On a production floor an immediate action might be to shut down production or stop shipments.

In development it's a little different, because you don't have to stop developing. Adjustments are made to handle the problem. For example, let's say that the system is not being backed up correctly. To fix this, developers might send a copy of important files to the server. Two developers might swap files of their work so there is more than one copy around.

Here are the activities that should be followed for immediate action:

- Clearly define the problem.

- Develop a team that understands this type of problem.

- Brainstorm.

- Develop an immediate action plan.

- Decide whether some kind of containment is needed.

- Decide who will work on the immediate steps.

- Decide who will review the immediate steps for completion.

- Notify the appropriate personnel.

- Set up the next meeting for temporary actions.

Not all findings need an immediate solution. If a document is missing information, development will not stop. If a programmer is not using the language standard, a plan could be developed to get the software to the standard before the product is delivered.

7.2 TEMPORARY ACTIONS

The temporary solution fixes the problem until a more acceptable permanent answer is found. Going back to our example, the developer might set up a manual backup system and perform this once a week. This is not the best answer because the backup will be missed if the person scheduled to do the manual backup is busy or just plain forgets. The software risk factor of the project starts to climb each time the backups are not performed.

Here are the activities that should be followed for temporary action:

- Organize the appropriate team or use the team from the immediate action.

- Investigate and verify the problem.

- Clearly define the problem.

- Present all known evidence.

- Explain the team objectives.

- Brainstorm the potential causes. If there is no permanent fix readily available, develop a temporary fix.

- Determine action(s) to correct the root cause for permanent action.

Some of these bullet items are repeated because not all problems go through the immediate phase.

7.3 PERMANENT ACTIONS

The permanent action makes the problem go away. In our example the development group buys a tape backup system that automatically stores updates daily and backs up the full system once a week. The only action involving a human is loading the tapes. No one needs to remember to do the backups.

Here are the activities that should be followed for permanent action:

- Use the correction from the temporary actions.

     or

- Organize the appropriate team, or use the team from either the immediate or temporary action.

- Investigate and verify the problem.

- Clearly define the problem.

- Present all known evidence.

- Explain the team's objectives.

- Brainstorm the potential causes.

- Determine action(s) to correct the root cause for permanent action.

In temporary and permanent actions:

- Implement action to correct the root cause.

- Verify the effect of the corrective action(s).

- Notify the appropriate personnel.

This problem should be documented and reviewed periodically to confirm the actions are still working and the problem is resolved. If the finding was a procedure, someone should check the results after a few weeks to make sure the team did not fall back into its old ways.

7.4 CONCLUSION

These three steps do not have to be followed to the letter. If a permanent fix is available immediately, you can skip the first two steps. But sometimes software must be written or a part or equipment must be ordered and you need a temporary step to keep things running.

Some clients want you to review the corrective action plan to see if you think it will fix the problem. You should read the plan and respond. It is not your place to come up with a better plan. If it becomes your fix, how would you be able to continue performing audits for this auditee? You might advise that the fix will work or that the auditee should rethink the fix, but that is as far you should go.

Make sure that there is a fix for the problem right away. Understand the three steps and use the first two. To illustrate, let's say that a back-up drive has been ordered and is scheduled to arrive in two weeks. Three weeks go by and still no drive. Meanwhile, there have been no backups as everyone waits for the new drive. The auditee cannot safely wait for the drive because they are opening development to a major software risk. If the system crashes, look at the time and resources it will take to rebuild the system.

The clients could ask you to review the corrective action results. You can review the results for face value. The only way you can confirm that they work is by an on-site mini-audit. Audit only the corrective action fixes. You want to make sure that the fix has relieved the problem and that it will continue to be used. Mark your records with the changes, the fixes, and the audit results. During the next audit with this auditee, review the corrective actions to confirm that they are still working.

Part III

Audit Constants

8

"Project" Management

If we look at the organizational chart in Chapter 14, we can trace from the software department's manager down to the individuals working on the project. But what about the outside forces dealing with development? These can include:

- Upper and middle management

- Accounting

- Human resources

- Project management

All of these people and departments influence the software project. If they work as a part of the team there is a greater opportunity for success. However, a mistake by any one of these can take the project down or delay it. Unless something comes up that points at one of them, don't spend a lot of time—a quick review is fine.

8.1 UPPER AND MIDDLE MANAGEMENT

There are only a few things that you can look at with upper management. This is because they may be the ones funding the audit and they also tend to close ranks. If the project is still in development, you need to know if they back the project. There are many things going on at this level that you as an auditor will never know. Talk to the manager one level above the software development manager or to someone who is not being held directly responsible for software. Remember that you need to know if there is a communication gap between the project and management. If you don't talk to both sides, how would you know?

The following questions should help you determine how much upper management knows about the project:

		What is your relationship with software development?
		What is your title?
		Can you list the software's problems?
		What is the next deliverable and when is it due?
		Is it on time?
		Why the delay?
		What is the next milestone?
		Do you receive status updates from development?
		Is the team over/under/right on budget?
		Do they work extra hours? Weeknights? Weekends?
		Are they allowed to work overtime?
		How would you evaluate the department manager? (one sentence)
		How often do you visit development?
		When was the last time you were in development?
		Do you ever attend a development meeting?

Do not make any announcements to the manager. If the manager says there are two problems, do not say, "You mean three." You want to know what the manager knows. Not all managers will know the next milestone if they are higher than one level above the department's manager. Budgets can be a driving force in a project. Management can stop overtime because of budget issues and overlook deadlines thereby causing missed deliveries.

8.2 ACCOUNTING

Accounting can supply valuable information about the project, including areas that are over or under budget. The budget is an estimate with normal variants, but when the numbers are way out it must be investigated. If the costs are under budget, the original requirements should be looked at to see if something was not included. When a part of the project is over budget, investigate for these reasons as well.

If the project is handled in one budget with no breakdowns, the total budget will not help. "Yes, we are over budget" means nothing. If the project is divided into phases, milestones, equipment, prototypes, or other details, the budget can be tracked.

Review the accounting reports that development is using. Look at them with open eyes and ask lots of questions. You want to know what the report means, where the data comes from, and how is it used. This is the only accurate indicator as to whether the numbers are factual and not estimated.

A word of warning about when an accounting department is running the project. They are so bottom-line focused that their decisions are budget oriented. Cutting manpower because the project is over budget is *not* always the right thing to do, but cutting manpower because the people are no longer needed *is* the right thing to do.

Some questions to use for the accounting department:

		Who is your accounting rep to software?
		How is accounting tracking this project?
		How is accounting getting the data?
		What reports is accounting producing?
program manager		What do you get from accounting?
		Who gets the reports?
		May I have copies of the reports?
		What does accounting do if the project goes over budget?
		How old is the data used in the reports?
		How is the data reported to management?
		Are exceptions to the budget tracked?
		Are the exceptions tracked passively or actively?
		Can accounting supply custom reports for the projects?

Confirm that the development manager is getting the reports, and ask what he/she is doing with them. How are they useful to him/her?

Look over the reports that accounting gives you, because they are a good source for questions in other areas. See how many of the reports are understood by the people receiving them. It's been my experience that accounting reports are the least likely to be read. At best, they tend to get a quick glance at the bottom line that is then quietly ignored in pursuit of the product development.

8.3 PROJECT MANAGER

Per *Juran's Quality Handbook*, "(a) project is a task which is undertaken in a structured manner. A project organizes the task and its proposed resolution into a structure in which there is a clear definition of the undertaking and the corresponding plan for its execution"[1]

Projects can use a significant quantity of the company's resources, including personnel, hardware, labs, materials, and other assets. The project manager is usually someone outside of the software world. (Sometimes the software manager is also the project manager.) The project manager will work with the software manager, designers, analyst, customers, facilities management, and any other people who would impact the project. All these stakeholders will give input to the project manager, who will put a plan together for scheduling. The stakeholders review the plan and request changes. Questions to ask:

		Is the project manager part of the development team?
		What is your title?
		Who do you report to?
		Who updates the schedule?
		Who do you report delays to?
		Do you make a schedule of the project?
		Do you use a project management package?
		How long have you been a project manager?
		Have you ever worked on another software project?
		What was the time frame of the original project?
		How often do you meet with the development team?
		Do you poll groups between meetings?
		Do you talk to suppliers? Who does?

---

[1] Juran and Godfrey, ed., *Juran's Quality Handbook,* 5th ed. (McGraw Hill, New York 1999), 17.1

		Do you track resources?
		What resources?
		Where did you get the milestones you used in the schedule?
		How did people giving you the milestones justify their timing?
		Did anyone shorten the schedule after it was completed?
		Do you work with accounting?

9

Schedule

The scheduling is another variable that can make or break a project. It sometimes provides the best view into the development cycle. The schedule is the project management tool that shows how a project is progressing. It could be one of management's most powerful tools, yet most people treat it as a place to store due dates. The schedule can mislead people into thinking that the project is going perfectly until the delivery date arrives and the project is not ready. Problems would have shown up before the delivery date, if the schedule were used correctly.

A quick overview of scheduling: The schedule is created with input from all parties and tracked by the project manager. Once the final date has been established, the project is divided into smaller segments called milestones. These milestones, which are steps toward the final date, could be a deliverable, an event, a completed task (a program, part of a program, design), or any other notable item. By cutting the project into smaller pieces, the project manager can track its progress.

Call it total quality management or big Q (quality overview of the total product), but scheduling is part of the quality system. When you read a schedule, use common sense. Putting the information on paper does not make it so. If the schedule shows that a team of five people will have a task completed in a month and you count only four people working on it, start asking questions. The subject of overtime will automatically come up. Ask to see time cards.

Some questions to assist you in determining how well the schedule is adhered to:

manager		Do you have a schedule?
manager		Who updates the schedule?
manager		How often does the schedule get updated?

manager		Is the schedule baselined?
manager		Do you have the original schedule?
manager		Does the schedule show any changes because of requirement changes?
manager		What is the next major milestone?
manager		Is any task falling behind?
manager		How do you justify the percentage of completion?
programmer		Do the managers help you with any problems?
programmer		Do the managers create a mitigation plan for large delays?
manager		Is the right quantity of scheduled people working on the task?
manager		The resources show five people working, but I see four. Why?
manager		How are they making up the time to complete the task?
manager		Are people actually working overtime to finish the task?
manager		Will they miss the date?
manager		If they are working overtime, are they getting paid?
manager		Are there time cards or a time sheet showing overtime?
manager		How will paying overtime affect the cost of the project?
manager		Why does the schedule need to have overtime?
manager		Is the project understaffed?
manager		What will the effect be on the rest of the project if you remain understaffed?
manager		What do you do about staff vacations and the schedule?
manager		What do you do with customer change requests?
manager		Does the schedule impact the approval of change requests?

In scheduling, if a project is being measured in years and someone asks for another year because of a problem, you might need to give it to them. If a project is being measured in months and someone asks for a month's extension, that could be all right to do. Likewise, if the project is measured in weeks or days you can choose to extend them the week or day. But when someone on a project measured in weeks asks for months then there's your heads up that something really big happened or someone was not being truthful with updates. This is a fundamental project management problem.

Can something happen just before a milestone, putting off the schedule for a month? Yes, but it had better be for a good reason. A missed or delayed milestone could cost or delay the auditee a milestone payment. This kind of issue is in the contract. I once saw a prototype machine go up in a puff of smoke because of a short caused by a dropped screwdriver. It cost the project a month. Thank goodness there was enough time left in the project to recover and meet the deadline.

The schedule is the thermostat of the project. You can see how well the project has been planned and how accurately. People make mistakes, and there will always be something changing on the schedule. The customer could request a change that might impact the schedule. This does not make it a bad project. A well-planned project will have some flexibility built into the schedule. If the team develops a good mitigation plan to get back on schedule, they are handling any potential schedule problems. Watch for the "perfect" project and take a good, long look. Nothing is perfect. Frequently a project that's perfect-looking is an indication of creative writing or good intentions gone awry.

Another place to look at is how many change requests, or just simple changes, the customer gets approved by the auditee. Note how many of the requests changed the schedule. It is not uncommon that the product changes but the schedule doesn't. This is especially important when there are milestone delays with nonpayment or reduced payment clauses.

The IEEE 1058 Standard for Software Project Management Plan[1] might give you insight into how the auditee set up the software project management. Understanding the plan helps you find missing elements in the schedule.

9.1 TYPES OF PROJECT MANAGEMENT SYSTEMS

There should be a detailed schedule dividing the major events into smaller traceable pieces. Usually 30 days after a contract is signed, a schedule is due. If there is no schedule and it has been longer than 30 days, you need to show this as a risk. This is a ship without a chart. There is no direction as to what has to be

---

[1] IEEE std. 1058–1998 Standard for Software Project Management Plan.

done and what is needed to get it done. You need a checklist of what modules are needed to complete the project.

Convert handwritten schedules into Microsoft Word or with a project management software package, making them easier to maintain. There should be a milestone for each of the steps to project completion.

Automated tools such as Microsoft's Project and Visio, Primavera's Sure-Track, and Artemis can be used to track the project. Each program has its own features. The main view is a Gantt chart (Figure 9.1), which shows all the milestones. They have an optional area that can be used for resources, personnel, equipment, and so on. All of the figures in this chapter (except 9.5, which is Visio) were originally made with Microsoft Project because it is widely used. The other tools might have small differences, but the charts will be fairly similar.

Once you have the schedule, find today's date. An example of the way to mark the day is in Figure 9.3. Now you know where the project should be and the names of all the documents/modules with their due date.

To understand the project management tools, you need to be able to read the charts. By starting with the simplest charts and continuing through more complex charts, this chapter will build a schedule using one set of data. Not all companies' tools look the same, but the same information is captured by each.

There are a few things you should know about automated project management tools. Each line is a task with a starting and ending date. The starting date can be entered with the days to completion and the tool will calculate the ending date. This is the simplest form.

9.2 SIMPLE CHARTS

In Figure 9.1 we can look at Part C (line 4) to see that it will last two days, Monday and Tuesday. If we look at Part A, we can see it will last seven days. Note that on my chart I allowed the weekend to be included in the calendar, but not the day count. You can see where each task fits into the overall project. This tool rolls up all the individual tasks into a header line, which will show the total time.

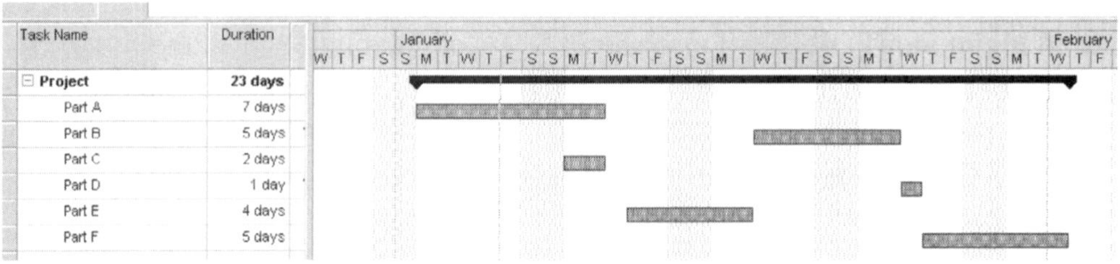

Figure 9.1 Simple chart.

Pick a few tasks on today's date and ask:

manager		Is this task completed?
manager		May I see the completed task?
manager		What date was it completed?
manager		When was it peer reviewed?
auditor		What date is on the actual completed date in the schedule?
manager		Is the documentation complete?
manager		May I see the documentation? (later ask for the peer review)
manager		Was it peer reviewed?

Pick a few tasks on the right side of today's date and ask:

manager		Will this task get started on time?
manager		Who will do this task?

9.3 INTERDEPENDENCIES

Most projects are more complex than the simple form. There are dependencies, such as you cannot write a routine to store data in a database until the database is defined. There is a column in the schedule task area that is called Predecessors. In this column is the number of the task(s) that must be completed before this task can begin. The project management software will draw arrows (Figure 9.2) from one box to another to show dependencies. Part B cannot get started until Parts A and E are finished. If any part except Parts A and C were delayed four days, it would affect the ending date.

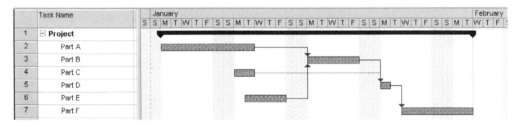

Figure 9.2 Interdependencies of tasks.

Look at Part A. It ends on Tuesday and there are Wednesday, Thursday, and Friday before Part B begins on the following Monday. If Part A or C were delayed a week, they would also stop Part B from starting. In Part D you will see that a day between Part D and the beginning of Part F has no assigned task. A gap like this in the schedule can be caused by having no resources available to do the task.

It is not unusual to find a hundred or more lines on a schedule. Dependencies can become a real workout to follow. Depending on how the schedule is set up, you might see that a red line connects tasks; this is the critical path. (There is more about critical path later in this chapter.) Follow the red line and ask about each task for that line:

auditor		Have you found any tasks without dependencies?
manager		Why are there tasks without dependencies?
manager		Is this task needed further along in the project?
manager		What happens if the task before this task is delayed?
manager		How is task information handed off to the next task?
manager		Can the next task get started without the entire last task completed?

When there is a delay in the completion of a task, review the names of the people working that task. Someone might be working more than one task at a time, which is doable unless they are scheduled for eight hours a day on each. This is another hole that needs to be researched.

9.4 PARTIALLY COMPLETED

The project management tools allow the percentage of completion to be entered. The project manager would simply ask "How much of ABC is completed?" The answer would be XX percent. Inside the bar will be a black line (see Figure 9.3) showing how much of that task has been completed. If you follow today's date down with the black line, you can see whether the project is ahead of or behind schedule.

I added a line to show today's date, but most packages will automatically display a line. This line makes it easier to see the short and long lines. A good place to start your questions would be about the longest and shortest lines from the date line. Of course, if all the lines are perfect on the date, something's really

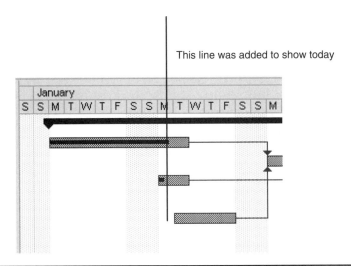

This line was added to show today

Figure 9.3 Partially completed chart.

wrong. No project is that perfect. One reason could be that the tool is not being used correctly. Some questions to ask:

manager		Why is this task behind (or ahead) of schedule?
manager		Why do all the percentages in the tasks line up to today's date?
manager		When was the last project update?
manager		Why is everything lined up to the update?

A good project manager will try to track the individual tasks. This is difficult to measure; the manager relies on his experience with the person doing the task. It takes only one or two tasks to give any person a track record. If in a project meeting, the project manager (or whoever updates the schedule) asks the person what percentage has been completed, an auditor's red flag should go up.

Think about your boss in a bad mood, and then imagine a room full of managers and peers. It is your turn to say how much more is complete. You know nothing new has been done, so what do you say? Right! 5 percent more; who can check 5 percent? Of course after 20 weeks your 100 percent is up and the task had better be complete.

If you think that you are not getting the whole story about the project, make a note of any tasks that are to be completed during the audit. At the end of the audit, ask a few open questions about that task. If the scheduled task is not completed during the audit, the schedule might be a piece of fiction.

> I attended two schedule meetings for a company's largest project. It was a multiyear, multi-million-dollar project. The room was arranged with tables creating a large square so everyone had face time. About 20 programmers, the director of software, and top managers were attending to question any slip of the schedule. At the second meeting, I figured out the 5 percent increase tactic described above. Management seemed to be very happy with the progress of the project. Why not? Everyone reported progress! The project failed within 18 months. The company paid back all of the deposit and step payments to stay out of court.

If the project scheduling meeting is a high-pressure meeting, where there is yelling over slips in the schedule, start digging deep for a misquoted schedule. Project schedule meetings should be low key, where if someone says that they fell behind schedule, the manager will find out what can be done to help the programmer:

manager		Tell me about the schedule meetings.
manager		How many people attend?
manager		Are there any upper level managers at the meetings?
manager		Who runs the meeting?
project manager		Does anyone miss a completion date?
project manager		How big are the tasks (days, weeks, months)?
project manager		Does the schedule slip at all?
project manager		Who do you report to?
project manager		Is hardware included on your schedule?
project manager		What outside components would affect the schedule?

You should have the answers to most of the above questions before the interviews by reading the schedule. However, it doesn't hurt to verify your conclusions and use the schedule as documentation for your final report.

9.5 BASELINES

Microsoft Project has an option (go to Tools, Track, Save Baseline) to lock the original schedule by setting the baseline. Then if there are any changes to the project it will show up on the schedule (Figure 9.4).

If the schedule has been baselined, you can find the slips by going to View, Track Gantt, and you will see two bars for each task. The actual bar is on top and the bottom is planned. The blue lines are on time and the red are not. Part A is the normal task completed on its due date. Something in Figure 9.4 was delayed two days; we needed to change Part E's start date from 1/10/06 to 1/12/06. Now you see the top lines on all of the dependent tasks have moved to the right two days. Remember the free day between Part D and Part F? Well, it disappeared. The schedule used it to make up one day. If the delay is in the critical path, you will see the final date move; otherwise you might not see the slip.

> I was attending project management meetings on a project that was getting close to the delivery date. The project management information was projected on a screen so that everyone could see the updates. After a few weeks I noticed a pattern developing. Engineer A had task XYZ to complete. His milestone for the completion was May 1. When May 1 arrived, the task was incomplete. On July 1 he completed task XYZ. The people who updated changes made the percentage of completion 100 percent. The completion date was never changed to July 1, which would have made all the dependents move to new dates. When you looked at the chart everything was on schedule.

When the problem with the date was finally fixed, a new problem was created. When the dates were changed, the charts became messy, so the person updating

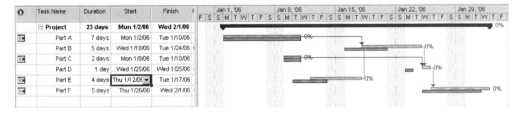

Figure 9.4   Baseline chart.

the charts started performing baselines each week. This would fix the charts and everything looked on time again. Some questions to ask:

manager		How often do you baseline?
manager		How do you show a delay?
manager		Do all tasks take longer than planned?
project manager		When do you tell the Software manager of slips in the schedule?

9.6 CRITICAL PATH

The project management must identify the critical path. Once each task has been defined and links are established, a map should be drawn from the first task to the last to identify the schedule's critical path. Tasks are arranged in a sequence. Each task needs to be completed before the next begins. All of this information is shown in the project schedule. Automated project management packages usually have a critical path option. The critical path method (CPM) diagram is a planning and tracking tool.

Here is a point that sometimes gets confusing. There is a difference between something that is really important to the outcome of the project, such as the creation of special data or a program completion, and a critical path task like meeting a deadline and receiving payment.

In the CPM diagram (Figure 9.5) the schedule is shown with the relationships between elements. For example, C can't start until A and B are completed. Let's

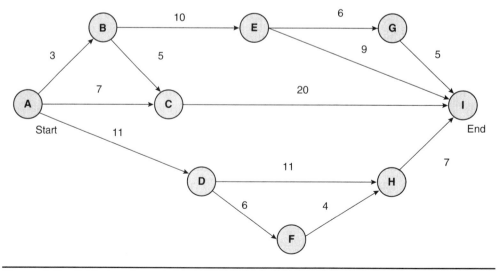

Figure 9.5   Critical path method.

see which path is the longest. We use the number of days between the two letters to calculate the days to completion:

A–C–I	8 + 20 = 28 days; C cannot start until B is complete
A–B–C–I	3 + 5 + 20 = 28 days
A–B–E–I	3 + 10 + 9 = 22 days
A–B–E–G–I	3 + 10 + 6 + 5 = 24 days
A–D–H–I	11 + 11 + 7 = 29 days
A–D–F–H–I	11 + 6 + 4 + 7 = 28 days

A–D–H–I has the greatest number of days, so it becomes the critical path. C could be the hardest part of the project, but if it takes an extra day the schedule would not change. Delaying the task could change the critical path. If the time between A and C is delayed by four days, the new critical path will be A–C–I, which would change to 30 days. Some questions to ask:

manager		Does the project have a critical path diagram?
manager		Do you track the critical path?
manager		What is your critical path?
manager		Show me the critical path.
manager		Has the critical path ever changed?
manager		When there is a slip of the schedule, is the critical path checked?
manager		Are suppliers' tasks on the critical path?
manager		How do you track other companies' tasks on the critical path?
manager		How much lead time did you give the other companies?
manager		Are other departments in your company tracked?
manager		How detailed is your plan?

The project management tools show a more detailed diagram than shown in Figure 9.5. In MS Project, it is called the Descriptive Network Diagram. Figure 9.6 is a view of the project that we have been using throughout this chapter. The details in the boxes cannot be read, but you can see the flow. If the diagram were in color you would see that the boxes in red are on the critical path.

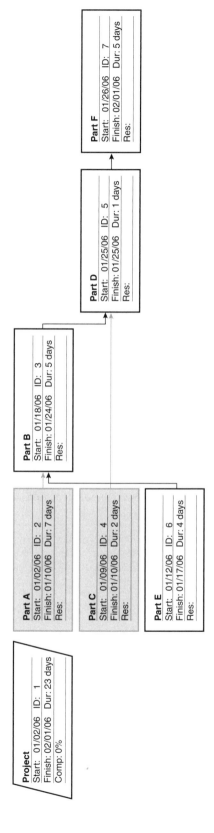

Figure 9.6 Descriptive network diagram.

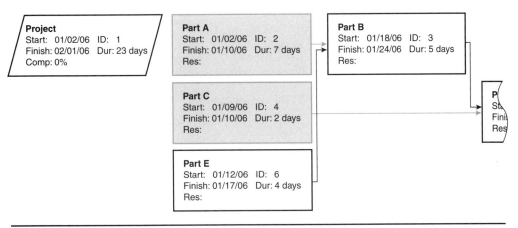

Figure 9.7   Enlarged descriptive network diagram.

Figure 9.7 is an enlarged copy of the first few boxes. The parallelogram on the left was missing from Figure 9.6 to allow the other boxes to fit on the page.

The parallelogram has the top-level name and ID (line number) of this view. On the next line, the duration and completed percentage are shown. The last line is the planned start and finish date.

The top line of the task box shows whether the task is in the noncritical or critical path of the project. Again, the box will be red and the connecting line is bolder if it is on the critical path. The next line is the name of the task and the ID number. The third line has the duration and completion percentage. The fourth line has the planned starting and ending dates. The last line has the resources for this task.

9.7 MORE SCHEDULE POINTS

Some of the project management tools give the user an opportunity to develop a resource planner. In this planner, personnel and equipment can be scheduled. This can be a good tool, and it can be a manager's worst nightmare. If you are presented with this option in the package, keep an open mind and evaluate it on the way it is being used.

Another option from the project management tool is costing. If you are not specifically working on a cost research audit, don't spend a lot of time reviewing it. This feature could help plan the budget, but it is only a starting point:

programmer		How do you report your task completion percentage?
programmer		When do you have schedule meetings?
programmer		Who attends the schedule meetings?
programmer		What happens when you are delayed?
programmer		Is there anything outside of your work that can delay you?
manager		Is testing included in your schedule?
manager		What happens the last day on the schedule?
manager		How often do you baseline?
manager		Do you track resources?
manager		May I have a copy of the resources report?
manager		Do you hold a formal review on each major milestone?
manager		Do you hold a formal review with each phase change?
manager		Does your customer see the schedule?

*Ask for attendance sheets and minutes

The top of this group of questions is for the programmers, not the manager. These are confirming the answers or opening new areas for questioning.

10

Project Status Reports

If any issues arise in development, there are two factors to think about. The first factor is the issue itself, and the second is the communication about the issue. It is a good idea to review the previous six or more months' project status reports from the project manager to management. If the project does not have a project manager, the role falls to the software manager.

You are looking to see when the issues were reported to management. If the issues have not been reported, you will need to follow down the status report chain to see where the reporting stopped. You will also need to find out what kind of plan was made to correct the issue.

By reviewing the project status reports, you will see what has been going on during the project. When were issues reported at the project meeting and to whom were they addressed? Questions to ask:

		Are there project status reports?
		Who writes the project status reports?
		Who receives the project status reports?

Here are some questions for reviewing the status reports:

		Do the reports show any project issues?
		Were the issues resolved during the meeting?
		Was someone assigned the issues?
		Was the issue on the agenda at the following meeting?
		What did the person report at the next meeting?

		Was the issue resolved and recorded?
		Was a mitigation plan developed?
		Is/was the mitigation plan traced in a timely manner?
		Was the mitigation plan completed?
		Were the results of the mitigation plan "as expected"?
		Who was notified of the issue and the mitigation plan?
		Was it approved by management? Who?
		Did management request updates on the mitigation plan?
		Did management use the project status for updates?
		Did any issues come up during project meetings?
		Were issues recorded?
		Were delays and why they occurred recorded?
		Were issues that could affect a milestone reported?
		Was the project meeting told at the milestone that there was an issue?
		Were delays or time slips written up?
		Does the time slip also explain the causes?

You are auditing two things here. The first is whether there is a system in place for reporting to management, and the second is whether it works. There can be delays on every project; if everyone understands the delays it's not a problem. Management finding out about a problem a month after it was originally found is a major company problem.

11

Configuration Management

What is configuration management? In its simplest form, it is document control. Software development has many pieces of documentation. Here are a few examples:

- Requirements
- Reviews
- Documents
- Software programs

In short, every document that is used to develop the software product must be controlled. Why controlled? Because there will be many people involved with developing the software. Each person wants to work from the latest copy of the document. There are software configuration control packages available to be used that allow a document to be checked in and out by any user. These packages will keep a history of the document and allow one person at a time to check out the document. When that person has made his changes to the document, he checks the document back into the package. By keeping the history of the software code, most packages will allow a recreation of an old build.

Let's talk about the three main functions of software configuration management. They are:

1. Configuration control—Controls the software modules, allowing the modules to be checked out, checked in, updated, and archived.

2. Change control—Controls the tracking of findings and changes to be made, and it has a configuration control board to approve the changes.

3. Version control—Controls the released software, what modules are to be included, and how the release is being built.

These are simple definitions. If you go to the standards listed earlier, you will find definitions in each. These are explained in more detail later in this chapter.

There are different standards for configuration control. Some might be useful to you, so I have included a brief description of each:

- ISO 10007 is not about software at all. However, the general rules are easily applied to software configuration.

- In IEEE/EIA 12207.2 Standard for Information Technology,[1] Sections 6.1 Documentation Process and 6.2 Configuration Management Process explain some of the suggested IEEE configuration controls. The Annexes of the Standard supply some software information:

  - Annex E Life Cycle Data Objectives

  - Annex F Use of Reusable Software Products

  - Annex G Candidate Joint Management Reviews

  - Annex H Software Measurement Categories

  - Annex I Guidance on Development Strategies and Build Plans

- IEEE std. 828 Standard for Software Configuration Management Plan[2] will give the auditor a good reference if it is needed to review the auditee plan.

Configuration control is essential to a software project to control the hundreds of documents generated when building the software. Projects can fail because the wrong configuration was delivered to the customer or the wrong version of software is inside a product. If the software is overseen by a regulating agency, the agencies could force a full recall of the product, which might be very costly to perform.

Even with a configuration management system in place, you will need to audit the procedures to assure that the configuration control system is updated to the latest version of the documents. The goal is to stop the wrong documents or software from being used or released to the field or customer. Everyone who handles files in the control system must follow the proper procedures for the function they are performing.

There are tools that can handle most of these software configuration controls. Many controls come together to create a total system. This chapter will cover the following areas:

- Document control

- Baselining

---

[1]IEEE/IEC 12207.2—1995 Standard for Information Technology—Software Life Cycle Processes—Implementation Consideration.
[2]IEEE Std.828—2005 IEEE Standard for Software Configuration Management Plan.

- Software configuration control

- Configuration control board

- Incident tracking

- Incident contentment report and analysis

- Backups and recovery

- Formal release

- Field configuration control

11.1 DOCUMENT CONTROL

Many problems can occur with documents. The more documents, the more problems. Let's start with an example so you understand the reasons for the audit question. Documents are written by different people during the start-up of the R & D project. Most managers control the initial document development. Now people start updating and modifying the documents. Someone adds a function to the functional specifications; it now is part of the document. This is how software documents were handled in the past. Everyone had their own copy of a document with their changes and not everyone else's. The result is chaos and lost data.

Let's look at an ideal document control system. As soon as a draft has been written, the document should be part of configuration control. At least once a week the document should be filed in the database and withdrawn again. A draft revision number should be used; the file is backed up automatically. If a developer or manager needs to look at the document, he just checks out a "view" copy that cannot be changed, secure in the knowledge that he has the latest version.

All documents that are used to develop some part of the system—(spreadsheets, presentations, charts, and sample databases)—and would be needed to reconstruct the development, should be saved in a version control package:

manager		Do you have version control?
manager		How does it work?
manager		What documents are under version control? (list the documents)
manager		May I have a printout of the version control directory and subdirectories?

manager		Can we trace back one document and look at the updates?
auditor		Does the directory show different version numbers?

The government and some commercial customers want documents baselined (explained below). This means that the document needs a change request before a change can be made. This request goes to a committee or a single person (if set up this way) for approval to allow the changes. Without the approval, no changes can be made. Here are some questions to determine whether the auditee uses change control for documents:

manager		Does the company use change requests (CR) for documents?
manager		(Yes) May I see the last 10 CRs?
manager		Are there any rejected CRs?
manager		Do the CRs have a project impact area?
manager		Is there a reference to schedule impact?
manager		Is there a reference to the cost of the change?
manager		Does the committee chair (or single chair) sign the CRs?
manager		Is the CR clear with supporting details?
manager		Does the CR specify when it will be in the system?
manager		Is there a list of all the programs affected by the CR?
manager		Is there a list of all database or interface changes?

Look for rejected change requests to prove that the committee is not rubber stamping the requests. The impact area on the form should be filled out before going into the review with the customer. Review the change request for incomplete data that would stop the customer from reviewing and signing off. If the customer requested the change, there might be a charge on it; but if it fixes an auditee problem, there should be no charge.

11.2 BASELINING

This is not the same baselining that we used in scheduling. The term baselining in configuration control is for software. Baselining the software is taking the first cut of the software to be tested and making a copy of all the source code into the configuration tool. From this moment on, any changes to the software must be approved by a software control committee or software manager.

When a software problem is found, the problem must be submitted to a problem tracking system. This is covered in section 11.4, "Incident Tracking."

Some companies will baseline each time they release to the field so that it cannot be changed by anyone. This release is frozen forever, and any changes will mean a new version number or letter.

A big advantage to baselining the code is that a programmer can temporarily add his code to the baseline and test his routine or changes. Working with a known baseline system keeps programmers from wasting time chasing someone else's error. Questions to ask:

manager		Do you use baselining?
manager		How does it work?

11.3 SOFTWARE CONFIGURATION CONTROL

This is where configuration control (version control) starts. All software that is in the system and supports the system must be under control. Here is a partial configuration control list:

Documents—These support software development.

Source code—This is the written code of the program.

Object file—This is the file that is created when a program is compiled.

Build file—This is the script that creates the object files and links them together.

Database schemas—Database layout files and descriptions.

Development tools—Compilers, editors, debuggers, and so forth.

The test for this area is whether there is control for all files that create the system. If after you build the software from the configuration area, someone says they need to add a module, table, or library, there is an error in the build script. Those components should have already been included. Unfortunately, the build file is usually the file that is overlooked. The true test of software configuration control is that years from now you will be able to rebuild the exact same release and it will match the original release down to the last file.

If there are flowcharts, object-oriented files, strawman, steelman, and other objects used in the system, they must also be under control. Development tools are

version number in the file or a date, the length will not change. If there is a checksum, you can compare them to be 100 percent certain they are the same.

11.4 INCIDENT TRACKING

Incident tracking (sometimes called bug tracking) is an important part of a complete system. While a computer package is ideal, here is another scenario that is more cumbersome but gets the job done. A person finds a bug while running a program, writes down the problem on a piece of paper, and gives it to the software manager. The software manager gives it to the programmer who wrote that program. After the programmer fixes the problem, he gives the paper back to the manager to have it retested. The manager or tester tests the bug, and if it is fixed the bug is closed. If not, the process starts over. On an audit a few years ago I came across a modern version of the paper system: the programmer had sticky notes stuck all around his monitor.

A paper system is better than *no* system for tracking problems and can be put in place in seconds. As soon as a paper system is in place, ideas start to flow. Prioritize by numbering the papers so the programmer knows which to correct first. Add the name of the person who found the problem and the programmer will know who to go to for more information, and so on.

Here is a point that needs to be cleared up: Bugs go by many other names—"problem" and "incident" to name two. Anything that requires correction, even if it is a customer requested enhancement, is a bug. You will come cross many different "bugs"—they all mean the same thing. The reporting forms could be called:

- Bug report (or bug sheet)
- Incident report (incident sheet)
- Change request
- Change order
- Software change request
- Software problem report

Now there is software to track every type of change to the system. The main purpose of the system is to make corrective action traceable. Once it has been recorded, it will remain open until someone closes it. Closing it means it has been handled, tested, and recorded. Questions to ask:

manager		What do you use to track problems?
manager		What kind of metrics do you get?
manager		Do you track anything other than problems? Explain.

There are all sorts of metrics that can be put together from the information included in a tracking system. It is not unusual to find open incidents listed as completed, having to be reopened because the problem was not fixed properly. Different companies handle bug reports differently. Some say they have no incidents reopened, but they open new problem reports. Numbers can be worked in many ways. Please read all the metrics with this in mind. Be aware: no matter how they dress it up, it's still a bug and they are having to take a second look at it.

The incident is tracked by logging it and testing upon completion. There is a mountain of data that can be captured about the incident:

- Incident ID

- Date found

- Time found

- Who found it

- Type of incident—logic, interface, performance, external, clerical, test, enhancement, new ideas, new request

- Level (priority) of incident—major, medium, low

- Which group (designer, programmer, tester, acceptance testers, and so on) found the incident

- Which group (specification writer, designer, programmer, and so on) caused the incident

- Description of the problem

- Additional set-up information (steps to problem)

- The phase in which the problem entered the project (bad spec, bad doc, bad code, and so on)

- Description of fix

- Version that fix will be installed in

- Status of incident

- Who fixed it

- Which other modules this problem affects

- List other modules changed

- Who reviewed changes?

- Who tested changes?

- Time required to make the changes

Other fields also could be used in this record. This should be tailored to the company's development. The important point here is that it makes no difference if this system is only on paper or computer as long as there is a central place to find outstanding problems, to record new ones, and to track their disposition:

manager		May I get a printout of the incident report?
homework		Is there enough information to track the incident?
manager		Are all the needed fields filled in?
manager		Is the description clear enough to understand the problem?
manager		Is the name of the person who found the problem listed?
manager		Is there enough room to record the whole incident?
manager		Is the fix recorded clearly and honestly?
manager		Is the incident tested after it is fixed?
manager		What happens if the incident fails the retest?

Put yourself in the shoes of the programmer. Can you understand the problem and where to start looking? Make sure the incident report is not too wordy or lacking pertinent information. I've seen programmers go in the wrong direction for hours on a poorly written incident. Sometimes it becomes necessary for the tester to recreate the report by writing each step (including the data used) to verify the incident. If you need to get to where the incident occurred, you have to step through several windows. When going from one screen to the next some testers use shorthand like this:

Main menu ⇒ Customer ⇒ Edit ⇒ Phone number

or

Main, Customer, Edit, Phone Number

When a company has multiple development teams and uses a tracking system for each, there must be some type of linking. If the general ledger team finds bad data coming from the accounts payable team, they must have a way to pass the problem to that team. Plus, they would want an incident report for their records showing what they found.

Here is a potential problem with multiple tracking systems. If different groups—that is, testers, automated testers, integration testers, and hardware testers—are checking out the code, you need to know what they are using to record the problems and how they are getting the incident report into the rest of the system.

If the company wants a cost of quality metric, the incident report is the place to start. Tracking the time to "fix" and test the problem, and entering the data on the incident report, makes this simple. With the high number of reopenings, this is a gold mine for cost data.

A tracking incident should start as soon as someone touches the code. There are companies that do not record incidents until after the first baseline. If a programmer sees a problem and there is no procedure requiring him to record it, then we have a major risk in development. It is a waste of time to find the incident a second time and then fix it. A complex program could have a million different paths through it. What happens if the incident found before the baseline is not recorded and that path never gets tested? After the system is delivered and the customer finds the problem, how much will it cost to fix?

Some forward-looking companies allow their sales people to use the tracking system to record their ideas for a new product or upgrade. These ideas or enhancements are reviewed before the next update of the system. The sales people are the voice of the customer to development, so their ideas are logged.

11.5 INCIDENT REPORT AND ANALYSIS

Okay, the incident is recorded and fixed. It's also been tested and closed. Now what? What information and lessons can the company learn from the reports? Is the company even looking at out-of-date incident reports? If these were analyzed, incidents could produce a flood of information.

By analyzing the incident reports, we can build a chart that management can utilize to make decisions about development.

A simple matrix can be drawn to do this analysis. Down one side write the names of functional groups from which incidents come, such as:

- Sales people

- Specification writers

- Designers

- Coders

- Integration/testers

- Performance testers

- Acceptance testers

Across the top list the groups or functions that find incidents, such as:

- Specification writers

- Designers

- Coders

- Integration/testers

- Performance testers

- Acceptance testers

The grid in Figure 11.1 is a simple layout to find out-of-normal work ranges. If a number stands out, take a close look.

If the auditee does not have this type of analysis, see what else they are using.

They might need to filter out the sales numbers. Make sure that no other data is mixed in with the incidents or this will not work. Also, if the grid is used, watch for large gaps between where the incident was introduced and where it was found. The wider the gap, the more costly fixing it may be. For example: an incident found in performance and introduced in design. Questions to ask:

manager		Do you perform incident analysis? Explain.
manager		What are the results of the analysis?
manager		Does one area stand out?
manager		What needs to be fixed from this metric?

Here's what the chart will show:

- Which function introduced the problem?

- Which function found the incident?

- Timing.

The company is looking for the function (shown in the following list) that introduced the problem and the group that found it. When the group finds a problem in

		Who Found It					
		Spec.	Design	Coding	Integration	Performance	Acceptance
Where	Sales						
	Spec.						
	Design						
	Coding						
	Integration						
	Performance						
	Acceptance						

Figure 11.1   Incident analysis grid.

the same function that introduced it, the cost stays at a minimum. Whoever found the incident tells the company how long the problem was in the system by noting in what phase it was introduced. The more phases, the more costly.

Two points need to be defined. First, consider the rules for what incidents go into which box. Everyone must use the same definitions. Second, a large number out of phase (that is, not found in the same phase as created) is only an indicator that there might be a problem. More research must be performed before any conclusions are drawn. Ask for large numbers to be explained.

How old is the data being analyzed? The time span is a factor. The sooner you discover an incident, the sooner you can institute a fix and the lower the attendant costs will be.

Watch out for "feel good matrixes"—the ones that give a false sense of security. A report in your hand is not useful unless it contains analysis and/or a conclusion:

varies		Does the report trace back to the source?
		What is the conclusion from the report?
		Does your conclusion match the analysis results?

11.6 SOFTWARE MEETING OR BOARD

This section has a very wide range of options. At the beginning of the range, the software lead can assign the problem report to his programmers informally, with no meeting. At the other end, the problem can be reported to a formal configuration review board. Since they meet weekly and then would need time to evaluate the problems and assign someone to fix it, this is often the unwieldy route.

A good software lead knows his/her people and the problem that needs to be fixed, and can assign the work and review the results. This is usually a small group of five or less programmers. Larger groups of programmers require more process to show how the work is distributed and checked after completion:

manager	1	How do you assign the problem reports?
manager	2	How do you track who has what?
manager	3	What happens when the programmer says it is done?
programmer	4	Who assigns the work?
programmer	5	Do you do your own debugging?

programmer	6	Does anyone check your work?
manager	7	What happens when something new is added to the project?

Questions 3 and 6 look for independent eyes or testing. Putting in a "fix" with no testing will lead to trouble later on.

Question 5 looks for team debuggers. Sometimes only one or two people do the debugging. We have only one debugger question:

debugger		When you find the problem, do you explain it to the programmer who wrote the code?

Question 7 looks for traceability back to the proposed change and how it impacts time and budget.

Cost and schedule changes then go to management for approval. With everyone in agreement, the document and all of the supporting documents are changed. Questions for additional changes:

manager		Are additions to the system reviewed?
manager		Are cost and budget changes reviewed? By whom?
manager		Does the customer approve the changes?

On the formal side, a board meeting quality record must be created including meeting minutes, attendance list, date, time, and location. Software boards are used only to authorize changes to the software modules. After the problem goes into review, is evaluated, and assigned to the right person, the fix is presented to the software group. The software board provides a forum for discussing and assigning work and keeping lines of communication open. Quality assurance oversees that the problem is being handled correctly and according to the processes defined. The board also has the power to authorize a release or to stop one. If necessary, the board can raise a problem to management for help or clarity.

For a deeper look into the company's software board, ask for a copy of the last software board agenda. Then ask for a printout of open items for the past year. Compare the agenda with the list of open items, they should match. However, in most companies you will find that open items are not always on the agenda. If they are not reviewed, they are quickly forgotten. Remember each software correction report is a bug or problem that is found in the system and, if not fixed, will be in the next release.

manager		What is your system for version numbers on documents and specifications?
manager		What does it take to change a specification after it's been approved?
manager		Can you show me the control document that lists the latest version of each document?
manager		What is your system for version numbers on software?
manager		Does each module within the system have its own version number?
manager		Can you show the last system release with all the modules' version numbers?
manager		Can you explain the version number?
manager		Can you show the last change to the system version number and the modules that caused the change?
manager		May I have the last 10 problems entered into the system?

11.7 BACKUPS AND RECOVERY

It is an Information Technology (IT) function to back up the systems, but not all companies use IT departments or third-party companies. Verify that they are current on backups.

No one speaks about backups until something happens to the system and data is lost. To illustrate: a company spent over 10 weeks to get a handle on what they lost when the system disk crashed, and another 3 months to rebuild it. This was a huge waste of time and resources.

On one audit, I asked about backups and was told that the system was completely backed up each week, with daily changes backed up daily. They assured me they could prove this was so. I believe that the software manager thought it was being performed. Later, it was found that his server was never put on the company's backup list. During a morning audit meeting he was told about the error and his chin hit the table with a bang. A week later I received proof and a thank-you note.

Here are a few common reasons for not having backups:

- Tape write/read error.
- Ran out of backup tapes.
- Tapes never show completion.
- The IT night shift handles it.
- Corporate IT does it every night.
- The back-up disk drive is full.

Most people that work in the computer industry can give you stories about backups. You should know that losing data is costly, and you want proof that it is being backed up. Do not accept someone's word; you want proof.

Here is the hard part. Has anyone ever tried to build a system from the backup? It would not be the first time that a company could not rebuild their files from the backups. Every few months, there should be a partial or whole test of the rebuild function. The test could be run on a different server. The test would not affect development.

Another problem with backups is when a PC's disk goes down. It could take a week or longer to rebuild it. Most of the time is spent finding the tape or disk that particular PC's data is written on. What structure is used to back up personal PCs?

manager	1	Do you run backups?
manager	2	When are your backups run?
manager	3	What media do you use for backups?
manager	4	How do you handle the backup media?
manager	5	What do you do with the backup media?
manager	6	Do any backup media go off site?
manager	7	Where do they go?
manager	8	How often do you change media with new replacements?
manager	9	Are the individual PCs backed up?
manager	10	Have you rebuilt a system from your backups to test it?
manager	11	Do you use son, father, and grandfather system?
manager	12	Where are your dailies stored?

manager	13	Do you have a log of the backups?
manager	14	Let's see the media and how it is labeled.
manager	15	Has anyone rebuilt their PC from the backup?
manager	16	How long did it take to find the data on the tape?
manager	17	How did the PC work after being rebuilt from the back-up?

Let's talk specifically about some of these questions.

If the answer to 2 is "no backups," mark another risk.

Question 4—Check if they are leaving the backup media in the machine.

Questions 5 and 12—Look for the routine. Are the media stored in a programmer's desk, file cabinets, fireproof safe (best option), or off site (another great option). Can it be damaged during storage?

Questions 6 and 7—Determine if one of the media sets leaves the site. Don't leave all media in the same place because of the risk of fire. Off-site storage could be another company building, the owner's home, or a bank vault. There are companies that will pick up and deliver the media.

Question 10—Most companies that do backups find out when they need to rebuild that they cannot.

Question 11—Find out whether three media sets are used to back up the data. This ensures that if one set doesn't work the others could be used.

Question 14—Checks the media labels to see what information is supplied. Is it daily or weekly backups? Does it have a control number, and is there a date?

11.8 DISK ARRAY FILE SERVER

Disk array file servers will store data. It is usually a five-disk array, and data is duplicated across the array. If one of the disks crashes, it can be replaced and the array system will restore the replaced disk. This is a great way to protect the data. The company will still need some sort of backup of the array—but this backup most likely would never be used. Some disk arrays can be copied during normal business hours without slowing the system. This backup can happen weekly with the tapes or media taken off site:

manager		Do you use a disk array for disk storage?
manager		How does the system monitor the disks?
manager		What happens when a disk fails?
manager		How do you know when a disk fails?
manager		Will the system automatically send an alarm about the failure?
manager		Do you need to shut the system down to replace the disk?
manager		Is the disk hot swappable (system stays on)?
manager		When would you do the replacement?
manager		Do you have extra disks here now?
manager		May I see them?
manager		Does the system get backed up?
manager		When does the system get backed up?
manager		Do you keep a log or file on backups?
manager		May I see the log?

Use the backup list for more detailed questions.

11.9 FORMAL RELEASE

To write about formal releases, a discussion about builds is needed. It does not matter if the build is for a banking system, Internet application, or a large enterprise system; the principles are the same. During the testing of the system, many builds are completed. These builds can be partial builds (components missing or incomplete) used to test the system at the present point. When the software team feels they have a deliverable package, there should be one pre-release build completed. This pre-release is a dress rehearsal of the final build. A list of each of the modules included in the release is used to audit the pre-release. At this time, all of the testing should be rerun to check whether it all works together. If no incidents or problems are found, either the pre-release or a formal build can be the official release build.

When the team commits to a final build, they put a version number/letter on the product. The final list from the last build should be used to build this release copy. A list of every component, including the name of the module and its version number/letter, must be recorded. This is the part that sets the system to be recreated at a later date and shows that the team has control over the software. An audit should be used to make sure all the components have been put in the software control database.

It sounds like a lot of extra testing, but a software package that goes to the field has the company's reputation riding on it. If one line is changed, the version number/letter must be changed and the previous build voided. This prevents different versions from having the same number/letter. Watch out for the one-line changes; a long list of major problems comes out of the "It's only one line" pitfall. Questions to ask:

builder		Do you create a pre-release version for testing?
builder		Is the pre-release completely tested?
builder		Do you have a list of each component with its version number?
builder		How do you mark the pre-release so people know it is not complete?
builder		What is the average number of pre-releases completed before the release?
builder		Do you allow one-line changes without retesting?
builder		Have you loaded the pre-release version over an existing system?
tester		Does the software work after overlaying the present system?
manager		Are there special programs to be run before a new release is installed?
tester		Have these special programs been tested?
manager		Will the customer be informed to back up their system before the installation?
manager		Does your company send installers to load the new system?
builder		Do you use the component list to build the release version?
builder		Does anyone check your work?
tester		Do you rerun the test after the release version is created?

builder		Do you ever reject a release version?
builder		Can I see a copy of the voided release?
builder		Do you create a master of each release?
builder		What do you do with the master copy?
builder		What do you put into version control after the build?
builder		When the release version is completed what do you do with it?
builder		Who do you send the final version to for release?
builder		Who do you notify that the release is ready?
builder		Is a copy of the release software put on a CD or DVD for storage?
manager		Does an information release go along with the software?
manager		Are the manuals updated to reflect the changes and new features?
builder		Is it stored in the same PC or in a closet with test builds?
manager		Who creates the copies for release to new customers?
manager		Are the copies serial numbered?
manager		Does the serial number get put on the released media?
manager		Does the installer place a copy of the serial number on the PC?
manager		Is there an installation script to install the software?
manager		Has it been tested?
manager		Has it been tested over old versions?
manager		Does it change the system configuration during updates?

11.10 FIELD CONFIGURATION CONTROL

Let's assume that the software is being sold all over the country and there are hundreds or thousands of copies in the field. There are two ways to track which software is installed at each customer site.

The first is that the revision or version is cut with only one configuration. Any change to the software bumps up the version number. This version number is what software companies use to track what is out in the field.

The second way of tracking is a little more complicated. Companies buy items from vendors to be delivered with the system. To illustrate, let's take a bill collector device used in vending machines, ATMs, and self-service registers. The company sends you version A when your software is released. Now the government issues new $20 bills. The company could replace all the devices or load the new driver so that the new bills will work. They need to record whether each site has the new bill driver.

The company will need to know all the locations with the version A devices. This could be any device connected to the system. There might be special code written for one customer and other changes for another customer. This type of configuration system is a huge job, but it is necessary.

You need to figure out if the system you are auditing should have field configuration controls. The Food and Drug Administration, the Federal Aviation Administration, and the military require that the software configuration be tracked. This might be beyond the scope of your audit, but sometimes asking the question will spark the auditee to plan what it will do after the release:

manager		Do you track the software in the field?
manager		Is it required? By whom?
manager		Do you track the different field configurations?
manager		Can you contact all your customers?
manager		Do you use registration mail-in cards?
manager		Do you track complaints?

12

Software Quality and Continuous Improvement

Software quality and continuous improvement were initially not included in the purpose of this book, which is primarily about using audits to find problems. However, these two subjects are auditable areas and therefore have been added to make the book complete. They are not the drivers of a project, but they do support it.

12.1 SOFTWARE QUALITY

Quality questions run through the whole development process. At every step or phase, quality should be involved. Quality puts a second set of eyes on processes and procedures. As discussed earlier, when you have one person create the software and give it to another person to verify the checksums or load the programs, you have a quality procedure. Quality also checks to make sure that what the software and configuration say they are doing, is actually done. When quality procedures are in place and routinely used, it is less likely that a step in the procedure will be skipped.

However, just because there is software quality does not mean that it is good software quality. Continuous improvement of the processes and procedures is needed to keep up with changes in development and new methods of development. If software quality does not make changes, quality starts to fall behind.

One software quality process does not fit all software development. Even projects within a company will have different procedures for quality. They all start with the same guidelines, but they are different projects and over time they adapt to the application. Do not assume that if you find outstanding software quality on one project that it represents a company standard.

If the auditee's policy or plan shows that there will be a software quality person working with the development team, then you should find a software quality person on every project. If the project or programming manager says they do not need a quality person, write the observation. Of course, the software quality person should be independent of the development chain of command.

If the auditee's policy or plan makes no reference to software quality, ask who is doing the software quality checks.

Some companies use software quality sporadically; often in a cyclical pattern. When quality is low and there are many mistakes—wrong software delivery, lost data, software that worked during a build and cannot be reproduced—then quality surfaces as the major problem and the budget will be wrung dry to pay for it. When things are running smoothly, they assume they don't need software quality, so it is dropped or pared to the bone. Then, they encounter another set of bumps in the road and the cycle is repeated.

To focus on quality, start with these questions:

manager		Who is your software quality person?
manager		How many hours are scheduled for this project?
manager		What are the tasks for the software quality person?
manager		What are the different areas that they cover?
manager		What other project does the software quality person work on?
manager		How big are these other projects?
manager		How many hours is the software quality person here?

To determine the capability approach and thoroughness of the quality staff, use these questions:

quality		What is your background?
quality		Are you performing software audits?
quality		May I see the last three audit results?
quality		Are you proactive or reactive?
quality		Do you review data files?
quality		Do you attend software reviews?
quality		Do you manage the quality? How?
quality		Do you witness builds?
quality		What else do you do during builds?

quality		How do you verify that the software is correct during copies?
quality		Do you attend peer reviews?
quality		How do you ensure quality?
quality		Do you review all software problem reports?
quality		Do you check on the final build if all software problem reports are closed?
quality		What other tasks do you perform?
quality		Do you audit processes?
quality		Do you audit procedures?
quality		Do you have a copy of the work instructions or procedures?
quality		May I see them?

12.2 CONTINUOUS IMPROVEMENT

Continuous improvement (CI) is a steady effort to reduce waste in either time or resources, and is one of the harder areas to audit. An auditor is not present from the start of a continuous improvement project to the end. The auditor can keep his eyes open for obvious waste, but you really don't know the auditee so how can you be sure?

As with quality, please do not take continuous improvement for granted. CI gets a lot of lip service and occasionally a company will put together a CI event to inspire "out of the box thinking" among the staff. As a trained Kaizen facilitator I've worked with several groups to make changes to improve processes and procedures. It's a great opportunity to work with a manager or employee who is untrained in continuous improvement but sees waste and says, "Enough of this. We need to fix this."

Continuous improvement can be expensive, so companies tend to work with only one method: Six Sigma, Kaizen, Lean, Lessons Learned, Best Practices, or another method. They are all solid programs. Is one better than another? No. They all have their place, and every business is different. No matter what method is chosen, follow-through is key to *continuous* improvement.

In production, continuous improvement is simple to do, look at a process that is repeated hundreds of times, study it, modify it, test it, and do it. Simply put, this is a plan-do-check-act cycle. Some of these techniques have moved into offices now.

According to an article in *Quality Digest*, "Can We Improve Continuous Improvement?," 80 percent of all issues are repeat issues[1] and 80 percent of all issues are with conforming material.[2]

If the same problems crop up time and again, either something is missing or is not being followed in the process. The process needs to be reevaluated to find the missing step or changed so that what is being skipped cannot be. If the problem happens every time, can the steps be changed to force this "skipped" step to be performed, or do you add a checklist so that each step gets a check mark?

How do you audit continuous improvement? What do you look for? Do you ask about written procedures and how many revisions have been made? When was the last change? If you read a procedure, look for steps that might have been removed or combined, and then ask about it to check the response. If they agree that the change would work or is valid, question more about their CI. If you are witnessing a procedure being performed and it does not match the written procedure, ask about the difference. If the answer is, "We updated the procedure," then ask why the document wasn't updated. As this is clearly where they are not following the procedure, it will give you some insight into the updates being done and maybe to their version of CI. Questions to ask:

manager		When was the last CI project?
manager		How many people were involved?
manager		What was the CI project?
manager		Can I see the notes/minutes/reviews of the CI project?
manager		How much time/resources were saved?
manager		How did you prove the savings?
manager		Were the changes documented?
manager		May I see the documentation?
manager		Was a procedure changed?
manager		Was the CI project a success?
manager		Who came up with the last CI project idea?
manager		Do you know of a planned CI project?
manager		Have you seen a place for a CI project?
manager		Please explain it.

---

[1]Nick Van Weerdenburg, *Quality Digest* (February 2009): 40.
[2]Ibid.

Ask about CI projects in each area you are auditing. CI should be used throughout the development project.

13

Customer Satisfaction

Customer satisfaction is built on two-way communication and delivering what the customer wants and when. During the audit, you must ask about the number and type of meetings held with the customer. You ask, "What did the customer say at the meeting? Show me the minutes." If there is no dialogue, the customer will not be happy at the end of the project.

Now for the other side of the coin. What if the customer *is* talking and no one is listening? The easy road for development is to do their job and stay away from the customer. Customers can ask some tough questions and too much availability might lead to never-ending refinement and stalled forward movement. Developers say that customers don't understand software and they don't understand the systems, and those are good reasons to not work with the customer.

The more difficult road is talking to the customer, thereby making the customer part of the development team. Sometimes the development team might have to teach the customer enough about systems to help it be a member. Yes, that might cause some changes in direction, but at the end they will have a happy customer.

What happens when the software development team says there is no customer yet? If they are developing a new product to sell, your questions should be on the order of whose idea it is, what marketing research has been done, and who designed it.

> In my first programming job after college, I joined a programming team with seven programmers and a programming manager with over 10 years in the industry. He designed a system that would be "perfect" for the industry's customers. We worked on the project for approximately two years, which is 14 manhour-years or about 28,000 hours. When the project was completed, the company presented it at a

> trade show. It was not the company's star exhibit, but our system was the best seller for the company at the show. Within two months, however, we had lost every customer. The system didn't work the way the customers needed for their businesses. It turned out that the manager had never spoken to any potential customer to get their opinion. After the team met with a group of the original buyers, the system was redesigned and the changes took an additional nine months at a huge cost to our company.

Working in a vacuum can be costly. If there are no direct customers, the software team should find some and get them involved. It will pay off in the long run.

If the software team says they are not working with or talking to their customers, start writing. The communication link is broken.

During the whole audit, you should continually ask about the customer involvement:

		Who is your customer?
		Who is your customer contact?
		What is the phone number of the customer contact?
		Is the customer internal or external?
		Do you work with the customer?
		When was the last time you talked to the customer?
		Does the customer come here for meetings?
		Do you go to the customer's office for meetings?
		Is your customer happy?
		Does the customer understand the system?
		Has the customer been involved with the life-cycle changes?
		Are there minutes of your meetings with the customer?
		Were there action items from the meeting?
		May I see the list of action items?

		How are you tracking these actions items?
		Does the customer review the results of the action item?
		Do you have signed change requests from the customer?
		Have there been any disagreements with the customer?
		What was the disagreement?
		Please give me a list of meetings with the customer and the reasons for the meetings.
		When is the next meeting with the customer?
		Has the customer ever agreed to changes to the schedule?
		Has the scope of the project changed?

You are probably wondering if I would call the customer. I have never called an external one yet. I believe that by asking for the number and having the person think I would call, the half-truths disappear. These questions should be asked of different people throughout the audit.

The following are questions to focus on communication between the customer and the project:

		Who from the customer attends your meetings?
		Are they always the same people?

Write down each of their names. Then ask the following questions for each person:

		Does this person speak often?
		Does he/she ask questions?
		What is the person's title?
		Does this person listen or just keep talking?
		Does this person talk to anyone who doesn't come to the meetings? (programmers, designers, analysts)
		Can I talk to the customer who is working with you?

		When you talk to this person (the customer), what do they talk about?
		Do they ever complain?
		What do you do with these complaints?

Now the project people:

		Who from the project team meets with the customer?
		What is their job title?
		What questions does this person normally answer?
		Who makes the presentation to the customer?
		Does the person use projection slides?
		Can I have a copy of the presentation? (review homework)
		Who is the project's main contact with the customer?

Keep your ears open for negative remarks about the customer. If anything negative is said around you, it's safe to assume that a lot more or worse is said when an outsider isn't standing there. Don't let the remark drop, but don't attack the remark. Start with general questions and continue probing for more details.

Part IV

Audit Processes

14

Reviewing Software Documents

Every company has its own names for documents and specifications. This can lead to a lot of confusion. Here is where you need to figure out for yourself where each of the documents you have fits into the development time line. In this chapter, generic names are used and the first paragraph description will help.

In the question section in this chapter, note that the questions are being presented in preparation for the audit. This is not the audit. I have interwoven questions about the document along with questions to the writer of the document. When you write your checklist, the questions can be grouped more easily this way.

Any proprietary issues and confidentiality agreements should have been taken care of before you received the documentation for preparation review. If not, do it now to avoid a problem later.

14.1 THE GOVERNING STANDARDS

As expressed in section 1.9, "Hierarchy of Standards and Requirements," there are many standards. Most standards are written with ISO 9000, 9001, and 9004 as their foundation. There are many specialized standards that could guide or govern companies. You will be asked to audit companies that use no standards. The standards' fundamental intent should still be followed for the client's best interest.

When a standard is being used by the company, you have your guide. Most standards will make reference to other standards; you will need to follow these also. The date and version of the standards are also important. You need to work with the same date as the auditee is using. The company is not required to change when a standard is updated. Questions to ask:

document		Does this company follow a standard?
document		Which standard are they using?

document		What is the standard's date?
document		Are any of the referenced standards listed?

If the company is using a standard, you must know the standard and understand what the company is required to do:

document		Are the standard requirements general or strict?
document		Are the requirements clear or do you have to read into them?

ISO 9001 is the most common standard. Depending on what ISO 9001 the company is working from, there are additional software guidelines:

- EN ISO 9000-3—Quality Management and Quality Assurance Standards—Part 3: Guidelines for the application of ISO 9001 to the development, supply, installation, and maintenance of computer software, this treats all software as from a supplier.

- BSI BS ISO/IEC 90003—Software Engineering Guidelines for the Application of ISO 9001 to Computer Software. The clause numbering is exactly the same as ISO 9001, so it is easy to research.

Both guidelines take ISO 9001 to a software world. You are able to write questions directly from both guidelines. There are areas not covered in the guidelines that are included in this book. Outside of government contracts, very few companies use these guidelines. They are both good reading to garner a better understanding of the more formal approach to the software development process.

ANSI/ISO/ASQ Q9001-2008 Clause 4.2.2 Quality Manual states:

The organization shall establish and maintain a quality manual that includes

a) the scope of the quality management system, including details of and justification for any exclusions,

b) the documented procedures established for the quality management system, or reference to them, and

c) a description of the interaction between the processes of the quality management system.[1]

---

[1]ANSI/ISO/ASQ Q9001—2008 Quality management systems—Requirements.

14.2 QUALITY MANUAL

If the auditee is part of a major company, the corporation quality manual might reference the division quality manual. To audit, you need both. Quality manuals come in all shapes and sizes. They can be very professionally prepared manuals using ISO 9001 directives or they could be someone in quality's wish list of good practices. If the company is using a standard, it will be included in the reference documents.

The quality manual is a good place to look at the company's vision, mission statement, and quality objectives. These policies and vision statements should be quoted and explained therein. This is another place to find the company's direction. The auditor should be asking people during the audit what these are and what they mean, just to see if the ideals of the company are being followed. The auditor should verify whether the software team's performance reflects the aims of the quality policies and objectives:

everyone		What is the company's vision?
everyone		What is the company's mission statement?
everyone		What is the division's (business unit) vision?
everyone		What is the division's (business unit) mission statement?
everyone		What is the department's vision?
everyone		What is the department's mission statement?

Here is an interesting note. When you ask the preceding questions, they may read the answer off a wall poster, which is okay. This shows that it is available for all to see. If the workers can't answer the question, this is a finding. Upper management creates the vision and mission statements, which state the core values and direction of the company.

The quality manual should list any requirements from the standards that they want to exclude. There should be a reason or justification for the exclusion. It could be as simple as "We do not manufacture any goods for our customers, only software, and there is no environmental impact." Questions to ask:

document		Did you receive a quality manual?
document		Is it from the corporate headquarters or the unit you are auditing?

When the auditee is ISO 9001 compliant, the quality manual might have the principal points of ISO 9001 defined. As the auditor reading the quality manual, you should highlight or take note of the principal points. It should be divided into five major sections directly from the ISO 9001 standard:

Clause 4—Quality management system

    4.1 General requirements

    4.2 Documentation requirements

    4.2.1 General

    4.2.2 Quality manual

    4.2.3 Control of documents

    4.2.4 Control of records

Clause 5—Management responsibility

    5.1 Management commitment

    5.2 Customer focus

    5.3 Quality policy

    5.4 Planning

    5.5 Responsibility, authority, and communication

    5.6 Management review

Clause 6—Resource management

Clause 7—Product realization

    7.1 Planning of product realization

    7.2 Customer-related processes

    7.3 Design and development

    7.4 Purchasing

Clause 8—Measure, analysis and improvement

    8.1 General

    8.2 Monitoring and measurements

    8.3 Control of nonconforming product

    8.4 Analysis of data

    8.5 Improvement[2]

---

[2] ANSI/ISO/ASQ Q9001—2008 Quality management systems—Requirements

The clauses are divided into subtopics, and some of the subtopics are further divided. Under each of the clauses, there will be a written explanation on how the company is compliant, or they might point to a procedure.

ISO 9000-3 has the same numbering of the clauses. An auditor can do corresponding software coverage. ISO-9000-3 looks at the software as being supplied. This is a must if the company is following ISO. You would be helping the company for its next ISO audit.

Companies that do not use ISO 9000 standards might include some definitions and procedures in the quality manual and there might be a reference to other software guidelines. In these manuals they could use a watered-down version of the ISO guidelines.

Companies make money by producing and selling products. R&D has a small part of the overall budget; below 10 percent is usually the case. So you would expect over 90 percent of the quality manual to be about production. However, since production is the largest part of the company's business, it becomes 100 percent of the quality manual. If you ask about quality in R&D, they would agree that the quality is important, but not the main focus. They will tell you that the quality manual should be updated to cover it.

Anything you find in the quality manual that pertains to R&D must be followed—and it is your job to check. Be careful dealing with the quality manual; do not let production processes move into the software area. This could be a costly mistake. Review what management believes covers software, but watch for "it must fit here" procedures. This is a place for common sense. If the procedures listed in the quality manual are for production, you must highlight the problems that arise from using them.

If there is no quality manual, hopefully they are using company standards. If there are no standards to follow, you are in for a long hard audit. You have to use good practices to audit the software development system. This is a more difficult follow-through because people can argue your findings down to thin air without a manual or standards to judge against. Management has to understand the position you are in. You will need to explain why your findings are valid and the risk they face if they don't correct them.

If there is a quality manual, the company is trying to bring quality into the workplace. If you find anything that could improve quality, companies with quality manuals are more receptive to new ideas. Do not be surprised to see software development companies that do not have a quality manual. If no quality manual exists, ask about procedure or process manuals that the company uses; at least it will be a good starting point.

14.3 CONTRACTUAL DOCUMENTATION

After all the talk, all the bargaining, all the discussions, all the promises, and all the hopes, a deal is made. How all this happened does not change anything. It is what is written down on a piece of paper that starts the whole project. The developing company writes a sales order, proposal, or some other kind of agreement and the customer signs it. The agreement that is signed could simply be an intent to do the project. There will be other documents that will detail the project.

What you are looking for is the first official document and all supporting documents that describe the project. By official, I mean agreed-upon documents. Napkins from a lunch, notes during bidding, and wish lists are not officially signed agreements. You will also need to have any amendments added onto the project signed. All of these documents should be controlled and version identified. Refer to the configuration control section of this book for more information.

We will break the contract down into two parts. The first is the initial agreement. If the agreement states that the project will follow document "XYZ version A" you will need copies of both. Highlight all the requirements you find. You might end up returning to this document when you have a question.

The second part is the amendments. If there are any changes to the original agreement, they must be agreed upon and signed. Sometimes instead of an amendment, they will change the original document and bump the revision level. So instead of XYZ version A, you would now have XYZ version B. They can also change the original document to clarify some point that will not impact time or cost. You want to know that the time/cost analysis took place. What the company agrees to do or charges would be separate from the analysis. There might be other factors leading up to the agreement. Again, you need to see a signed agreement between the parties.

Generally, the military and government have taken amendments to an art form. These should be a model for all projects. Each time there is a change, they insist it be documented.

14.4 ORGANIZATIONAL CHART

Why in the world do you want an organizational chart? You need to know who you are talking to and where they sit on the chart. Second, you need to know who reports to whom. You need to see the dynamics of the department.

You will need one chart for the project and one to cover the software department. The project chart can give you a who's who of the project: the names and titles of all the players. See Figure 14.1.

Figure 14.1 shows you that Adam is Director of Software. Below him are three team managers of software. For this audit of team 2 software, you need to find the person who is responsible for getting the software completed. In this example, C. Conner is the software manager. You will also note that Gardener is the test lead and reports to Conner.

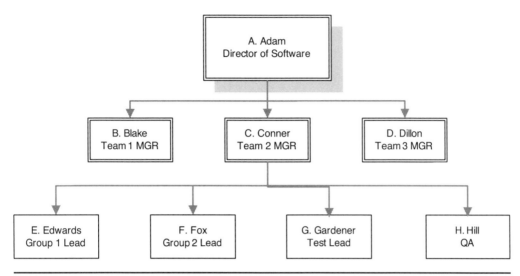

Figure 14.1 Software organizational chart.

Let's build a case study. Team 2 is scheduled to complete the code and unit testing in 10 months. The test group is scheduled to complete integration and testing in two months with delivery to the customer the following week. This is a total of 12 months. Team 2 has a few problems with the development and will need an extra month. Now the test team has one month to complete their testing. The test team spends two weeks working overtime to catch up and finds a new problem. The test lead, Gardener, shows the problem to his manager, Conner. If the programming team fixes the problem, the delivery date will be missed. Conner says it could be fixed in the next release, and Gardener believes that it should be fixed now because it will have a major function missing. The team is in conflict. Gardener fights for resolution but his boss wants the software out on time. Gardener depends on Conner for his next raise and to keep his job, so he acquiesces. The decision to ship is being made by a person protecting his job, not the project or company. This happens everyday and that's where an audit can step in, reveal the finding, and have it addressed.

If there is a quality assurance team or person, they will have the same problem. This all could happen without Adam, the director, finding out until the customer comes to complain. The flaw is in the organizational chart. Gardner should be answering to someone outside the team. Questions to ask:

manager	1	How is the software tested on the organizational chart?
manager		Is the testing independent?
manager	2	Do the programmers perform unit testing?

manager	3	Do the programmers do more than unit testing?
manager	4	Who manages the testers?
tester	5	What happens when you report a problem?
tester		How do you get along with the programmers?
programmer		How do you get along with the testers?

Notes for questions:

1. You want to know if there is independent testing. If there is no independent testing, it is a risk. If the manager says that there is independent testing, you will want to talk to the tester to confirm it.

2. Programmers should perform their own unit testing. If they don't, there is a waste of time and money on the little things that a tester will find.

3. This also confirms the independent testing. The programmers should not be doing any test above unit testing, but they can support it.

4. Does the tester work for the manager? Even if there seems to be no problem with this arrangement, it can grow into one.

5. You want to know if there is resistance to reporting bugs or errors.

manager		Is this the present organizational chart?
tester		Is this the present organizational chart?
qa		Is this the present organizational chart?

14.5 SCHEDULE

We can start with a definition of a project.

A project is a task which is undertaken in a structured manner. A project organizes the task and its proposed resolution into a structure in which there is clear definition of the undertaking and the corresponding plan for its execution.[3]

If the project has a good professional project manager, the schedule is a guide or reference. If the schedule shows that the project is on time, but you are audit-

---

[3]Juran and Godfrey, ed., *Juran's Quality Handbook,* 5th ed. (McGraw Hill, New York, 1999), 17.1.

ing because of a missed date, you should look into the schedule for details. If the schedule shows that the project is delayed, you know the communications to this point are correct and prove that the delay was known before the delivery date.

A project has three parts: a beginning, a middle, and an end. How the project gets from beginning to end must be laid out in a plan. The success of a project will depend upon the effort, care, and skill you apply in its initial planning. The plan should outline the steps needed to complete the project. The completion of each of these steps is called a milestone. Intraconnection between major milestones and their dependence on one another must be considered in the plan. When all the milestones are defined, the time it will take to complete each milestone is estimated. The time line that is created becomes the schedule. The schedule is a plan that is not cast in stone. Times can change and the schedule can change, but you need to know where the project is now and the impact expected from any changes.

The schedule is a view of the project management. You will need to know whether it is fact or fiction. Some projects use the schedule to cover the holes on the walls. Others will hang the schedule on the wall as part of their visual management plan. They let everyone know where the project is, what is expected next, and how their job fits into the whole plan. The schedule can be one of the most powerful tools, but it can also mislead with a false feeling of "all is well."

The places to look for errors in a schedule are:

- The total project—The person who makes up the schedule often focuses on one team and fails to see how it fits into the whole project. All the teams need to submit their tasks to be included in the schedule. It should be a team approach to develop the schedule.

- Communications within the project—There are many entities in a project, including software developers, testers, suppliers, and the customer. You can also have hardware in the mix on some projects. Each entity must define what they need and when they need it. There must be cross talk regularly. It can be time consuming at the beginning, but it will save major time at the end.

- Timescale—The times that appear in a schedule are best-case. There is no allowance for a problem or delay.

- Milestones—Are milestones defined in the requirement or sales agreement? What kind of reporting of the milestone is needed for the customer? Are there billable milestones, and how are they confirmed as being completed?

- External dependencies—The team's work may depend on other teams or suppliers. If one team misses its target date, it ripples to the final date.

- Resources—This category tends to be ignored. Everything needs to be thought out. How many people with what skills are needed? What equipment is required, and where will the work be done? One person cannot do two jobs at the same time at 100 percent efficiency. Is the budget realistic?

- Distribution development—This could be different teams at the same location or one team in different locations. This makes communication more critical. Who is doing what and where?

If you have received a schedule, review it and get a feel for where the project is at the time of the audit. There are more detailed questions in Chapter 9.

14.6 GENERAL DOCUMENTS DISCUSSION

You are now entering the largest source of errors in software, the documentation. These errors include: missing data, facts in conflict, badly worded and misunderstood specifications, and sometimes the biggest error—the documents are not read after being written.

We need to define a few words to help in reviewing documents. *May, should, can,* and *might* are optional words; when you see these words the requirement is optional. *Shall, must,* and *will* are mandatory words. Some companies remove all "shalls" and replace them with "wills" because there is less confusion.

You are reviewing these documents to give an independent and objective evaluation. You need to follow requirements from one document to the next without seeing any change in the meaning. You will need to be able to discuss the system with at least a good idea of what is being developed.

There's a lot of boilerplate and fluff used in reviewing specifications. Sometimes, I feel that the specifications are rated by the pound. But, better too much than too little. You need to be *Dragnet*'s Joe Friday, saying, "Just the facts, ma'am." Here is a method I use to review specifications. You will need a blank pad of paper and four highlighters of different colors.

Here is what I use the colors for:

- Yellow is for requirements. This is any statement that can be proven. For example, use the statement that the "first screen to appear is the login." The requirement is verifiable.

- Green is for communication interfaces with hardware or other software components

- Pink is for something not clear or TBD (to be defined or to be determined). An example of an unclear definition is "The program shall work like MS Windows." What does this mean? If we ask any 10 people, you will get 10 different answers. How about "The program shall work like MS Windows and find any menu within three clicks of the mouse." This is testable and can be proven to work.

- Blue is for references to other documents, which you will need a copy of to review.

The pad is for acronyms. Engineers and programmers use acronyms for everything. Each time you see a new one, write it down. The first time you see an acronym it should have the meaning included. This way you are checking for the same acronyms with different meanings. Some acronyms are standard, such as PS or ASAP. These are familiar to nearly everyone. You will, however, run across an acronym that you recognize and discover that at a different company it has a different meaning. Do not take acronyms for granted. The list will also be helpful during the interviews.

Other things that are critical and should be enhanced in each succeeding document are:

- Flowcharts
- Screen or report mockups
- Formulas or special instructions
- Interface requirements (I/O) and type (Internet, T-line, and so on)
- Distribution of processing
- Special and name devices included in the system

Depending on which phase of development you are auditing, you should see these documents:

- Software development plan
- Functional specification
- Software requirements specification
- Software design description (specification)
- Interface description
- Test plans (could be up to three plans or a three-part document)
- User documents (one of the last to be completed)
- Configuration management plan
- Software quality assurance plan
- Software safety plan

This is a wish list. Take what you can get.

14.7 SOFTWARE DEVELOPMENT PLAN

The software development plan describes a developer's plans for conducting a software development effort.[4] When a company is only developing one type of product, there may not be a software development plan. If the company is producing many types, you should see plans for each. These contain all of the ground rules for the project. There is a system overview, document overview, and many more details. You can audit the project from the software development plan with all the details that are presented. This is the document about *how* the project is going to be worked. This could include which tools should be used for the development, such as compilers, editor software, debug tools, and test tools.

At the beginning, the project might be missing some details, because some things might not be defined yet. As the project matures, more and more details should be added to the plan. Of course, some auditee will write this document once and never update it. Some will update it annually and some when the need arises.

Here is a list of some of the components to be included:

- Name of the project (any other basic data: Purchase Order number, and so on)

- Description of the project

- System and quality objectives

- Software life-cycle plan

- Any area in which a supplier might be used and for what

- Safety requirements

- List of the plans needed (quality, configuration control)

- Directions for peer reviews

- Overview of the hardware to be used

- Security issues

- Tools (or types of tools) needed

- Type of testing to be used

- Support and installation

---

[4]Software Development Plan (SDP) Di-IPSC-81427A dated 20000110.

14.8 FUNCTIONAL SPECIFICATION

The functional specification document could have different names:

- Proposal

- Statement of work

- Contract

Every company has different names for this document. We are looking for the document that describes the project. This is the document about *what* is to be done. We will call it the "starter" document because it is the document that officially starts the project. This document shows everything that is expected from the software including all the functionality. It might also show the delivery date, price (or budget), and any special milestones. Use these dates to check the schedule. If the schedule is different, find out why the changes occurred. This is the document that is signed by either the customer or the authority in charge, program manager, software manager, and (if they have one) test manager. Having all of these signatures shows that everyone acknowledges seeing the document and agrees with the contents. If this document does not exist, there is a major risk.

Here is a quote I have hanging over my desk:

Our plans miscarry because they have no aim. When a man does not know what harbor he is making for, no wind is the right wind.

Seneca (4 B.C–A.D. 65)

If the company doesn't have an agreement on what is to be done, something called "requirement creep" or "functional creep" may start to expand the project. When I worked in software, I found that you can come to full agreement with a customer, including the cost, and as you shake hands and head to the door, the customer will say, "One more thing." Hold on to your hat, because you are going to hear about a major addition. Be ready to start negotiating all over again. If there is no signed agreement from all parties, anyone can change the rules, at any time. New wishes get added on the fly, but the customer's required delivery date doesn't change. The company will not receive additional money to cover these changes. On the other side of the coin, programmers have been known to arbitrarily omit functions to make their schedule. Without the document, no one can prove or disprove what was to be done. Customer satisfaction will drop lower with each part missing or not functioning. Questions to ask:

manager		Is the "starter" document signed?
manager		Do you have a signed copy of the document?

In the case of a custom project, the functional spec could be developed from a proposal or statement of work that the company sent to a customer and the customer approved:

manager		Are there any amendments or notes (revision number/ letter) to show changes to the initial document that the customer approved?
manager		How much time were the stakeholders given to review the change?
manager		How many changes have there been?
manager		Any major changes?
manager		Were the changes signed by all parties?
manager		Were additional charges added to the original quote?
manager		How big was the impact on the schedule?
manager		Was an impact study performed?
manager		Who performed the study?
manager		May I see the study? (even if it was rejected)
manager		Did all stakeholders sign?

In the document, there are a few thing to look for and confirm. They are as follows:

Project Overview (could be Scope or Purpose)

This should be one of the first sections of the document. This section is a summary of the project at a 10,000-foot level. It should be clear enough for anyone (even a person who does not work in development) to understand. A block diagram could be helpful. Questions to ask:

document		Was the overview clear and understandable?
document		Could you explain an overview of the project from what you read?

Project Deliverables

This section should explain what will be delivered to the customer and the agreed-upon dates. It should include a list of milestones and what is to be delivered at them. It will also include items like a user manual and the training the customer will require:

document		Is there a project deliverable section?
document		What media will the software be delivered on?
document		Is one of the deliverables a user manual?
document		Will the product have a full help-screen system?
document		Will the system have a tutorial?
document		Will the software install automatically?
document		Will someone have to go to the customer to install the software?
document		Does the database need to be installed or loaded?
document		Who supplies any additional software (database, OS, and so on)?
document		Who pays for the additional software?
document		Are there dates for deliverables?
document		Are there milestone deliverables?
document		Is an acceptance test required?
document		Will the customer supply live data to test with?
document		Are there conditions for a delivery default?

Interfaces

Does the document identify the other software and hardware components required to work with this project? If there is special hardware being developed to work with the system, development will need the specifications for the device. Only a small percentage of today's software is developed to run on a PC. Most software written is to control everything from alarm clocks to space stations. All industrial software interfaces with something.

For example, look at cars produced in the last ten years. They all have software, from electronic ignition to global positioning systems. How many interfaces are there in a car? You will need the specifications to track down the interface protocols to receive or transmit information to different devices. Questions to ask:

document		Is there an interface description (specification) document?
document		What types of devices are being connected?
document		Who is writing the software for the devices?
document		Do you need to interface (or connect) to other software?
document		What type of connection is it?

Other Sections

• Priorities

• Objectives

• Assumptions

• Constraints

• Risk evaluation

Use the color system I described earlier to divide and highlight the areas important to your audit.

14.9 SOFTWARE REQUIREMENT SPECIFICATION

• Considerations for producing a good SRS

• The parts of an SRS

Robert Lewis's book contains overwhelming evidence collected over 30 years (written in 1992 and still true) that requirements documents are the weakest link in the software chain. And the worst part is that many times the developer does not know just how bad it is until it is far too late in the process to correct it without major impact to the program.[5]

ISO 9000:2005 defines *requirement* as a "need or expectation that is stated, generally implied, or obligatory."[6] A requirement can be a vague idea that the customer knows he wants but is unable to define. Sometimes the customer knows they need something but are not sure exactly how it works until it is developed. This is an open-ended requirement that development should get completely defined as soon as possible.

The auditee will write the requirements the way they understand them. The requirement should be correct, clear, complete, consistent, accurate, and testable. As an auditor, you might be able to check whether they are accurate without spending time with the customer.

> Complete—The requirements should cover all aspects and details. If you can think of an open end to the requirement, you have found an incomplete requirement.

---

[5]Robert O. Lewis, *Independent Verification & Validation: A Life Cycle Engineering Process for Quality Software* (Wiley Series in New Dimensions in Engineering, 1992), 112.
[6]ANSI/ISO/ASQ Q9000-2005: Quality management systems—Fundamentals and vocabulary.

Clear—All readers of the requirement should have the same understanding of what is to be done.

Consistent—The requirement should not conflict with another requirement or specification.

Testable—The requirement can be tested with clear results.

Let me paraphrase a great definition of software requirements: Specification is a set of requirements that, when realized, will satisfy an expressed need.[7] If the requirement is not in the document, it will not be in the final product. There should be a unique identifier (or you might add one) for each requirement; an example would be SRS100. This would mean it is from the SRS and is requirement 100. You will see more about this in Chapter 20, "Independent Verification and Validation."

Once the requirements have been accepted by all parties, they are put under configuration control. If additions or changes are needed, a change request must be submitted to and approved by a committee or board.

Changing a requirement can change the scope and cost of the project. If they are not going through a committee, you will need to write this as a finding. Here are some questions for the auditor:

		How were new or changed requirements entered into the system?
		Who approved the new requirements?
		Was there an impact study on the scheduling?
		Was a cost impact made?

As an auditor, you cannot tell what is missing from the specification unless you can compare it to the original sales document. If you have the original sales document, you might be able to trace the key parts of the project.

The biggest part of reviewing this document is to understand what is in the system and are the details clear. The details are clear if you can write a test to prove that this item is in the final product. Remember my example with the system working like MS Windows. Questions to ask:

		Is there a purpose or scope?
		Is the purpose or scope clear?

---

[7]IEEE Std. 1233—1998 Guide for Developing System Requirement Specifications, 1.

		Are there definitions and are they clear?
		Are there other documents in the references?
auditor		Do you have a copy of each document listed?
		Is there an overview of the project? Is it clear?
		Are the functions to be included defined? Are they clear?
		Are any constraints listed? Are they clear?
		Are any assumptions listed? What assumptions?
		Are any dependencies listed? Are they clear?
		Is there an overview of the system flow? Is it clear?
		Are the process descriptions clear?
		Are the overviews of the databases clear?
		Is a list of the databases needed for the project?
		Are the file descriptions within the databases defined?
		Are there preliminary layouts of the records for each file?
		Is each field defined within the records?
		Is the user interface defined?
		Are there preliminary screen designs?
		Are the output field descriptions defined?
		Are the software interfaces defined?
		Are the communication interfaces defined?
		Is the servers' hardware configuration defined?
		Is the users' hardware configuration defined?
		Are there performance requirements defined?
		(No) Is there a performance specification document?
auditor		(Yes) Get a copy of the performance specification document!
		Are there any other requirement sections?

There is an IEEE Std 830 Recommended Practices for Software Requirements Specification[8] (SRS) that has additional information.

14.10 SOFTWARE DESIGN SPECIFICATION

The design specification document formulates the software requirement specifications into an actual system. The design arranges all of the requirements for the system in a format where they will work together. There might be more than one way to create a system, but the design as it is mapped out is the way the design group feels it will work the best.

Each of the requirements that is added to the design should be labeled with either the unique identifier or a continuation of the SRS example such as DS100. This means that this is requirement 100 in the design specification (SDS). Every requirement should be traceable to the design document.

The design specification provides an overview of the system or project. Figure 14.2 shows an overview of an accounts receivable system. The arrows show the direction of the data flow. The diagram in Figure 14.2 shows that the system will interface with the accounting system. It also shows that invoicing and order entry will communicate with the inventory system. There is an Internet connection to the inquiry and order entry programs.

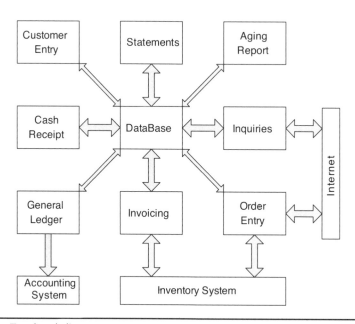

Figure 14.2 Top-level diagram—accounts receivable.

---

[7]IEEE Std. 830—1998 Recommended Practice for Software Requirements Specification, 3, 10.

Each of the arrows in Figure 14.2 must have interface information. Communication to the database is in the record format and the message header. The rest is done in two levels. The first is the network the message travels across between the boxes. The second is the actual format of the message. This should be described in the interface document. If there is no interface document, use their diagram as a starting point. Make sure they have all the interfaces between the boxes defined. Do not forget—in a double-headed arrow there should be two formats.

The system could also be completely contained on one circuit card (Figure 14.3) like the microwave system I designed for our discussion. Doing the diagram helps the designer understand the parts of the system.

The circuit card system is a little different from the PC system. First the communications are with hardware devices. Each device will have a different protocol (sequence of signals) to make the connection and to pass data. You are not going to understand each, or maybe any, of these protocols, but by the very means of asking to see them you will bring to the surface more information. When you look at the information, ask if it is working now. Unless you understand the protocol, ask no more questions.

With the overview under your belt, build your knowledge base diagram by diagram. This is a great help when you are asking questions:

		Is there an overview of the system?
		Is it a good starting point for the design?
		Has the customer seen this document?

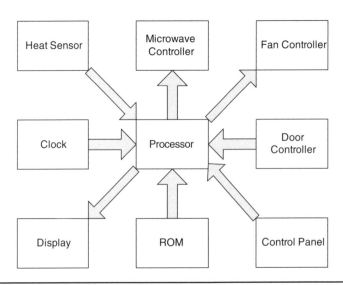

Figure 14.3 Circuit card systems for a microwave.

		Does the customer understand and agree with the overview diagrams?
		Is there a sign-off on the design?

Now in either the computer system or the circuit card system each succeeding box reveals more detail. In the case of the circuit card, the processor might be receiving data from a hardware sensor or hardware circuits. Then the design will show the interface between the sensor and the processor. Either the sensor will cause an interrupt or the processor will poll for input.

It is the same on the bigger systems. Is the system completely contained in one PC that includes its own database or is each box its own computer connected to a network database server in another computer? Each of these decisions makes a difference in the way the software must be written. One of the things you need to follow (if they are using a server) is whether the software is written for a server all the way through development. To decide to move it to a database server late in the project can be costly.

There are more block diagrams, data flow diagrams, and data views than I've described here. The person designing the system will choose the best way to explain the system.

In the new object-oriented world you will see a context view of the system (Figure 14.4) This diagram shows the same details as Figure 14.2 with the addition of naming the data going in each direction. For example, look at the top left corner of the view.[9] Customer Entry shows that the program could have new data input to the database. At the same time the operators can look up customer information.

In the design specifications, you might see a diagram of the classes used to build the system, as illustrated in Figure 14.5 using data from 14.2.

The auditor is looking for a clear design of the system. By looking through this document, you want to know that time was put into the design. If the design is not written out, the system is most likely being built on the fly. When the project was given to them to design, the ideas were flowing. However, after a year, things start showing up as overlooked or forgotten. Questions to ask:

		Do you see any gaps in the design?
		Was there enough description of the diagrams or charts?
		Do the other documents support this design?

---

[9]This diagram was originally drawn in MS Visio 2003.

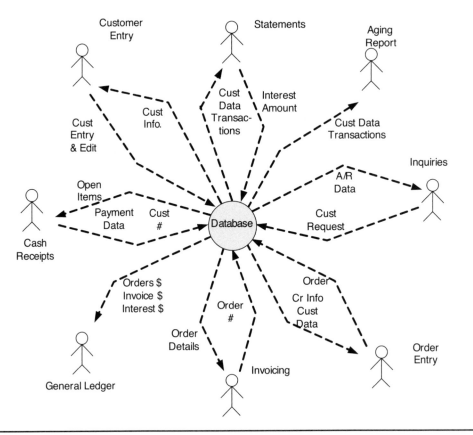

Figure 14.4   Context view.

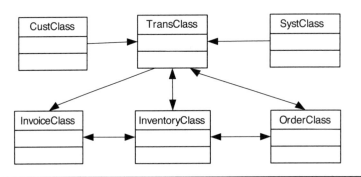

Figure 14.5   Accounts receivables classes.

Other diagrams that could be included in the design document are:

- Data flow diagram
- State transition diagrams
- Structure layouts

- Timing diagrams

- Entity relationship diagrams

- Sequence diagrams

- Network layouts

14.11 SOFTWARE CONFIGURATION MANAGEMENT PLAN

The software configuration management (SCM) plan documents which SCM activities are to be done, how they are done, who is responsible for doing them, when they happen, and what resources are required.[10] This is from the IEEE 828 Software Configuration Management Plan standard, which you can use for a guide for comparison.

This document could be a stand alone document or part of the software development plan. The purpose of software configuration management is to establish and maintain the integrity of the software documents (source code) and supporting documentation such as:

- Documents, specifications, requirements

- Design charts

- Test scripts

- Test results

- Anything that is written or drawn that would help to rebuild the development system

Some companies will put their documents in a document control system, and others will put them in the same system as the programs to keep it all in the same database. SCM involves identifying the configuration of the software at any given time during the development life cycle.

The plan describes what is to be controlled and how the versions or revisions are to be labeled. What artifacts from the software would also need to be tracked? In some systems the software and documents will be baselined, meaning that it is frozen at key points along the development cycle. Any changes to the baseline must be submitted to a configuration control board using a (software) change request. This is covered in detail in Chapter 11, "Configuration Management."

---

[10]IEEE 828 IEEE Standard for Software Configuration Management Plans.

Baselining software helps everyone on the project add their software to the working system to test their module. There will also be control of the software libraries and development tools. Questions to ask:

		Is there a software configuration management plan (SCMP)?
		Does the SCMP cover baseline controls?
		Does the SCMP define the version numbering/lettering?
		Does the SCMP define the product used to do the version control?
		Does the SCMP show a sample change request form?
		Does the SCMP define the bug tracking or problem reporting system?
		Does the SCMP detail how a build will be created?
		Does the SCMP detail the software configuration control board (SCCB)?
		Does the SCMP state who (by title) will be on the SCCB?
		Do you see anything that should be controlled but is not listed?
		Will the SCCB meeting be weekly or on call?
		Is this document under configuration control?
		Check all documents for revision labels.
		If a document is found with no label, is it under version control?

14.12 PERFORMANCE SPECIFICATION

The performance specification stores the parameters needed to run the system as planned. This specification could be in the software requirements or functional specifications.

This could be as simple as "the system will process and print 100 invoices a day" or as complex as "an Internet site able to handle a million hits per hour." You will find companies that have never actually calculated what they need in volume and whether the system can handle it. I have seen companies that have gotten to the end of the project only to find that the database could not handle the expected volume, forcing them to redesign the way the data is handled. No customer likes a missed delivery date.

There should be a means to calculate the throughput of the system at each stage and at peak times, with a safety margin built in:

		Is there a performance specification?
		Have you seen anything that could be used as a performance spec?
		Confirm the numbers during later interviews.
		Has the math been completed?

14.13 PROCESSES, PROCEDURES, AND WORK INSTRUCTIONS

Processes and procedures are general instructions about the order in which things are to be done. They are difficult to change in some companies because they come from a higher source such as company directives.

Work instructions are between the processes and procedures and the worker. These instructions are more detailed. The work instructions are easier to change because they are at a project level.

Here are examples:

Procedure—All software developed will be under version control and updated weekly.

Work Instruction—The developer will use Microsoft SourceSafe on the development server to save all programs.

		Are any processes defined?
		Are the processes clear and easily understood?
		Are there work instructions?
		Are the processes under version control?
		Are the work instructions signed and dated?
		Do the processes explain the details of a procedure?
		Are the work instructions under version control?
		Are the processes, procedures, and work instructions in an easy-to-find location?

14.14 TEST PLAN

The test plan defines how integration testing will be performed and scheduled it. These plans help figure out the resources needed to develop the tests, the resources to run the tests and the equipment needed for the testing. If the plan is laid out correctly, all the resources would be in the right place at the right time.

If equipment needs to be ordered in advance, this is the time to define the requirements for the test equipment or devices and order them if no special equipment is needed. It might be as easy as ordering the final configuration of the system. With all the above information, a budget could be mapped out early in the development process. Questions to ask:

		Are there test plans available?
		Do the test plans define the manpower to do the testing?
		Do the test plans show a schedule of equipment resources?
		Is special test equipment on order?

For more information, the IEEE Computer Society has written the IEEE Std. 829 Standard for Software Test Documentation. It includes:

- Test plan
- Test design specification
- Test case specification
- Test procedure specification
- Test item transmittal report
- Test log
- Test incident report
- Test summary

These are listed directly from the table of contents.

Generally, the test plan could run a little behind the rest of the development but should actually be started after the requirement specifications have been finalized. It is a real, living document at the beginning that grows during development.

The best-case test plan should list each of the requirements with the following items:

- Test number

- Requirement identification (SRS 100 or DS 100)

- Set-up instructions for the hardware

- Set-up instructions for the operating system(s)

- Set-up instructions for the data (preloaded for this test)

- Instructions taking the operator from a starting point to the test case for this requirement

- What the results should be

- Pass/fail check boxes

- Tester name and date tested

- Next test number from this point

14.15 SOFTWARE QUALITY PLAN

This plan details how software quality will be kept at its highest. There should be someone outside the development team to monitor quality issues such as builds, peer reviews, code reviews, and design reviews. They should also sit on the software configuration control board and monitor the processes, procedures, and work instructions.

If the company plans to be in business for any length of time, quarterly processes should be a major part of development:

		Is there a software quality plan (SQP)?
		Does the SQP define quality control details?
		Does the SQP indicate that the quality person be independent of the development team?
		Does the SQP detail all the planned areas the quality person will work in?
		Is the SQP easy to understand and doable?

A good reference for this area is IEEE Std. 730 Standard for Software Quality Assurance Plans.[11]

14.16 DATABASE LAYOUTS/SCHEMAS

The largest percentage of systems developed will have some sort of database. To review a database, you need to see the relationship between files and records. You'll need the layout of each type of record in the system.

---

[11]IEEE 730—2002 Standard for Software Quality Assurance Plans.

15

Peer Reviews

I believe that reviews make a group into a team. People on a project work like individuals until they are reviewing each other's work. When you put a group of developers together for a review, it creates a team. Every person sees where their work fits in the project and what others are doing that could affect their work.

In software development, the earlier a defect is found, the cheaper it is to fix. If a defect is found in the requirements stage of the project, the cost would be making the change and e-mailing the new copy out. To illustrate, let's say that the total cost is $200 to make the change. Now let's say the same problem is not found until testing. Using the sample graph in Figure 15.1, the unit of cost is multiplied against the cost of a defect found in the first phase. Now the defect might cost 66 times the $200, or $13,200, to fix because the code, design, and requirements all need to be changed. If the defect is found in the operation (field) phase, it could cost 158 times the $200, or $31,600, to fix plus the cost of fixing all the field systems. The unit of cost would need to be fine-tuned in any company depending on its procedures. It is not unusual for a change in the requirement phase to cost up to $500 because of the size of the project. Now, if you look at the problem during installation, the unit of cost is 100 times and the total cost is $50,000.

The greater the time between when the problem was introduced and when it was discovered, the higher the cost.

Reviews help find defects earlier. I have been collecting data on reviews and my findings are that 54 percent are clerical and no big deal. Now flip the percentage—46 percent are actual logic or coding defects. Many believe that it costs too much to have reviews; the answer is you can't afford not to have the reviews. Management should allocate resources and funding for performing peer reviews.

Here's another interesting statistic: I took 25 design and code peer reviews and found the average time to find one logic or coding error was 3.8 man-hours. The following box details how I arrived at this number.

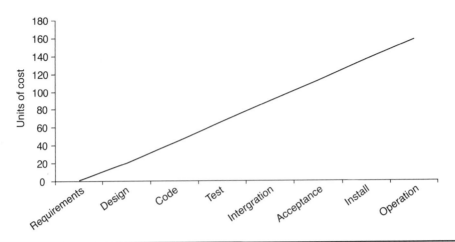

Figure 15.1 Cost of an error over the software life cycle.[1]

> Here is where the average comes from:
>
> At the beginning of each peer review, attendance was taken and the attendees were asked how much time they spent on studying the material. I filtered out the nonreviewers. Multiplying the attendee by the hours of the review plus the material review time gave a total time. I divided this total time by the total number of nonclerical findings. This was performed for each peer review.

Here is an actual review I attended.

> During audits, I like to attend a peer review. Some time ago I sat in on a code review. While the leader was going from page to page, the team was finding all sorts of clerical changes. These are valuable for software maintenance, but they are clerical. Finally someone pointed out a logic error. It took about five minutes of spirited discussion before the attendees agreed that it was a major logic defect. Afterwards, the manager shared with me that the defect would have taken months to surface and several weeks to fix.

---

[1]John W. Horch, *Practical Guide to Software Quality Management* (Boston: Artech House 1996), 48.

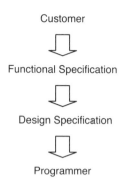

Customer

Functional Specification

Design Specification

Programmer

Figure 15.2   Information flow down.

Let's see all the places where a misunderstanding can occur. Figure 15.2 shows the flow of information.

When I was a kid in grade school, we played a game called "telephone." The teacher would whisper a sentence to a student, who would repeat it to the next, and so on. The last child would stand up and tell what they heard. Rarely was it anything but gibberish. Without a documented information flow down, the final product would have no resemblance to the customer's request.

During the audit, take a good close look at the peer review system. There is a good chance that not all findings in a closed review are closed. If a finding is in review, it is not closed. Each finding must have an explanation or resolution. Again, if it is not written down, it didn't happen.

Reviews keep a project on track. When people work in a vacuum, the project has a higher probability of failure. We are going to look at types of reviews.

15.1 PEER REVIEW BASICS

This covers all the peer reviews. If any of the following reviews are not performed, you have a risk. A peer review must be planned in advance. All interested parties including specialists should be invited. Reviewers should receive a copy of what is being reviewed with enough time to review it before the meeting. These peer reviews are a methodical examination of the document or code being presented. At the meeting, attendance should be taken and a record made of the amount of time each reviewer spent reviewing the item before the meeting.

Anyone can run the meeting, but you do need a good recorder. This person will keep notes of defects and capture corrective actions. The starting time, ending time, date, location, and name of the document/code with the revision number should also be recorded.

After the review, all action items must be recorded with the name of the person responsible for completing the correction and the due date. Each item must be tracked to completion. When all the items for each review are completed, the review is closed.

Here is a quick checklist for reviews:

- Compliance with standards and procedures

- Completeness

- Correctness

- Formatting rules

- Maintainability

Here are the generic questions for basic peer reviews (more detailed questions are in the following sections):

	1	Do you perform XX (fill in type) peer reviews?
	2	How many XX reviews has the software team performed in the last year?
	3	Please show me an invitation to the peer review.
	4	Was there enough time between the invitation and the review?
	5	Was the document included?
	6	Did the invitation have the time, duration, and location?
	7	Was a peer review held?
	8	Is there a list for a quorum?
	9	Was there a quorum?
	10	Was the attendance taken?
	11	Was the prereview time recorded?
	12	Were the corrective actions recorded?
	13	Was someone assigned to each corrective action?
	14	Was a due date included?
	15	If the corrective action is completed, was the date recorded?
	16	Is the peer review closed when all corrective actions are completed?

Follow this procedure with all reviews.

Note: If there is no quorum or specialists available, a peer review can be postponed. In fact, it is good to have records of a postponed meeting because it shows that the review was put on hold instead of canceled. This tells you that the review process is valued. It would not be out of line to invite the customers to a major review to keep them up to date.

Reviews are not personal; they are to help the project continue on track. If peer reviews are used as a stick to evaluate employees, they will lose support quickly. You should ask:

manager		Do you use peer reviews to evaluate your team members?

If the team is in two locations, don't let the peer review drop. There are now many ways to hold peer reviews with multiple sites. Dial-in conference calls are the easiest for multiple sites, or one meeting can make a conference call to another. It should be asked:

manager		Are you able to have a peer review at (all or) both locations?

Another point about peer reviews—they have a training aspect. New programmers learn how the more experienced programmers write code and comments. There is pressure to do a better job when they know that their peers are going to see their work.

NOTE: We are looking at the reviews, not the documents. Documents are covered in Chapter 14.

15.2 PEER REVIEW OF THE SALES ORDER

We are not looking at this from the legal or business perspective. We want to know if someone from development has reviewed the sales order before the company finalizes it. Development has given estimates of time and highlighted risks that might come up in the development. You are auditing this after the sales order was signed and work has begun.

This could be a custom system or modifications to an existing system. Sales people sell; their job is to get a signature on the bottom line. Some companies have technical people meeting with the potential customer to iron out the details. Others sign the order first and then see if it can be done. You want to know how the order (delivered to development) was handled:

		Was the sales order signed by the customer?
		Did a software person from development see the order before it was signed?
		Did software accept the order before it was signed?
		Was the sales order reviewed by development?
		Are deliverables listed during development of the software?
		What are the deliverables?
		Are they on the schedule?
		Who calculated the man-hours?
		On what do you base the man-hour figures?
		Does the customer understand the schedule?
		Did the customer accept the schedule?
		Did the software team point out any development problems?
		Do you have a software plan?
		Do you have the manpower to complete the project?
		Do you have the equipment to complete the project?
		Will there be ramp-up time?
		Is the ramp-up built into the schedule?
		Is any special or long-lead-time hardware on the project?
		Is any special training needed for this project?
		Was the training scheduled?
		Was the training completed?

15.3 PEER REVIEW OF THE SOFTWARE DEVELOPMENT PLAN

You are looking to see if all major players reviewed the software development plan. Often, only management reviews the plan. If a review by the key development personnel follows the management review, there is no problem. Management is looking at the project as a business decision. What would be the return on investment? How would this project advance the knowledge base of the company? Hopefully, key development personnel will highlight any problems:

		How many people reviewed this software development plan?
		Did the project manager sign the software development plan?
		Did the software manager sign the software development plan?
		Did the software team review the plan?
		Did the quality manager sign the software development plan?
		Did the hardware manager sign the software development plan?

Use the checklist in section 14.1 also.

This is where you ask the questions you developed from your review of the software development plan that you read before starting the audit.

15.4 PEER REVIEW OF THE REQUIREMENTS OR FUNCTIONAL SPECIFICATION

I think the most important document in a software project is the requirements or functional specification. This document is the agreement between the customer and development on what is to be produced. The budget and schedule are compiled from the requirements. Any changes must be approved by both parties.

Meanwhile, the list of people to review this document has grown. If the document was not approved, were changes made and was it reviewed again? Did they repeat this until *everyone* said they could work with it?

Here are the reviewers and what they will be looking for:

- Project manager—to calculate the schedule and resources.

- Customer—to see if everything they need is included.

- Software managers—the design and final product.

- Quality manager—the clarity of specifications and when there will be requirement checkpoints.

- Test manager—is each requirement clear enough and testable.

- Hardware manager—the interfaces to the hardware.

Each reviewer must sign off:

		How many people reviewed the specification?
		Did the project manager sign the specification?
		Did the software manager sign the specification?
		Did the software team review the specification?
		Did the quality manager sign the specification?
		Did the test manager sign the specification?
		Did the hardware manager need to review the specification?

After the software requirement specification has been signed, the requirements should go under configuration control and a change control board should manage the requirements. This is discussed in Chapter 11.

You are auditing the review process; the two main questions are (1) Was the document reviewed? and (2) Were the findings tracked and resolved? Everyone who signs the specification is agreeing that they can complete the work on time and budget. More details for what should be in the specification are in Chapter 14.

15.5 PEER REVIEW OF THE DESIGN PLAN

Now that the auditee has the requirement or functional specification approved, the next step is the design plan. In designing the plan the system architecture is included. Block diagrams and descriptions help to define the structure. Databases can also be defined in this plan. The interfaces start to become more defined.

You are auditing the peer review of the plan and must feel confident that they have an understanding of the design after reading it.

This phase of the process is critical if the team is using object-oriented development. The experience of the team in object-oriented development is a major factor. How high the learning curve is becomes a degree of difficulty. The object-oriented concept has come a long way since its rocky beginning and has become a powerful tool in software development. Several object-oriented modeling methods have been developed; most likely the modeling you see will reflect the time the development team started using it. Not every company will use object-oriented development exactly the same (just like any other development paradigm.)

		How many people reviewed the design plan?
		Did the project manager sign the design plan?
		Did the software manager sign the design plan?
		Did the software team review the design plan?
		Did the quality manager sign the design plan?
		Did the hardware manager need to review the design plan?

15.6 PEER REVIEW OF THE CODE

Code peer review (sometimes called inspections) can be a little tricky. Some programmers become very possessive when their code is reviewed. Code reviews are on the software, not the programmer. There are many ways for code to be reviewed. First, you want to know that it was reviewed and secondly how it was reviewed. Where were the findings recorded?

Here are some things that should be in the peer review:

- Code to a company standard.

- Code to a language standard.

- Too many comments.

- Not enough comments (depending on the routine).

- Are routine input/outputs explained in the routines header?

- Safety banner (if needed).

- Control structures.

- Check for only one exit from a routine.

- Are variables clearly defined?

- Coding conventions.

- Can someone else pick this code up five years from now and make changes?

- Is there a clear flow to the routine?

- Error handling routines.

- Is there a definition of the routine in the header?

- Programmers review the logic.

- What types of feedback are the programmers getting?

Review a few written meeting minutes and action items from peer reviews:

		Did everyone have prereview time?
		Are the findings listed clearly?
		Was the version number/letter on the code?
		Did the findings get closed?
		Was the point when the problem was introduced into the system noted?
		Is there a due date on all the findings?
		Was the type of finding listed?
		Was there someone assigned to each finding?
		Who will review the fix to verify that the changes fix the problem?
		Does the review show the version that these changes will appear in?
		Was any type of automated code analyzer used?
		What were the results?

There are many software code review tools on the market and more arrive every day. If the auditee uses one or more, review the findings and note what gets done with them.

15.7 PEER REVIEW OF THE TEST PLAN

The tester or test writer usually does not attend the programming team's meetings. They work from the functional specification to write the software. It is a good idea to have the software team review the test plan.

Check the reviews, findings, and comments, and use these questions:

		How many programmers attended?
		How much time was used to prepare for the review?
		Are the findings well explained?

		How long did the review take?
		Are all the findings closed?
		Was the meeting closed when the conference room time ran out?
		Was the review finished?
		Who reviewed the changes when closed?

This also shows how much time is being put into the testing of the system. If there is no plan, push for the test scripts. This could turn into a major project risk.

16

Hidden Software

Software management is responsible for the final software product. Many software managers do not understand the depth of this statement until it is too late. Software management is also responsible for software that is not developed by them but that is in the product or that could affect the final product.

For clarity let's call the software written in the software department the main software and everything else secondary.

Secondary software can be divided into two groups: direct software and indirect software. Both will affect the final product.

16.1 DIRECT SOFTWARE

This section highlights software that is physically connected to the main software. The simplest way to define secondary direct software is that they share a processor.

Here are a few examples of direct software and who could have written it:

Specialized drivers—written by hardware engineers

Interface routines for databases—written by database specialists and sometimes called scripts or stored procedures

Package software—supplied by an outside manufacturer and used by the main software team to perform a function

Protocols to specialize hardware—provided by a supplier's independent team

Operating systems—written by software companies

Do not accept any of this software as perfect. Even the operating system might not be exactly what the main software needs. Here is where you start to look for hidden software:

system engineer	1	How many processors are in your product?
system engineer	2	(Any number over 1) Do you write the software for each processor?
system engineer	3	(No) Who writes the software for that processor?
system engineer	4	What is the name or function for that processor?
system engineer	5	Are they part of this company? Another team?
system engineer	6	(Yes) Who is head of that group? (Audit that group)
system engineer	7	(No) Is it custom software?
system engineer	8	(Yes) Go to supplier section.
system engineer	9	(No) Commercial?
system engineer	10	(Yes) How do you test it?
system engineer	11	How much processor time does the software use? (Performance #)
system engineer	12	How much time does this software use?
system engineer	13	Who uses the difference? (go back to 3 for the next processor)

The two key points here are how many processors are used and who is using them. Even though there is one processor, the time could be time-sliced (shared) to someone else's software.

16.1.1 Specialized Drivers

The best way to explain this is by example. The software system runs a string of traffic lights. Each light works independently. The engineers who developed the interface to the hardware wrote a protocol that the system software could call. This protocol handles all the signals between the software and hardware. The main software transmits to traffic light X to turn green. The protocol finds the proper traffic light to signal the hardware to turn off red and turn on green.

Here are some questions for specialized drivers:

system engineer		What, other than PCs, does this system control?
system engineer		Who wrote the software?
system engineer		Is there a test plan?
system engineer		Was it tested?
system engineer		(Yes) May I see the results?
system engineer		What does this software do?
system engineer		What hardware is attached to the system?
system engineer		Can you name the driver for each piece of hardware?
system engineer		Are any of these drivers used elsewhere? (history)

When you get the drivers' names, track down who supplied them. Then dig into that supplier.

16.1.2 Interface Routines for Databases

Some systems handle their own reads and writes to the database. But there are times when the software needs to do extra functions when reading and writing. There might be queuing of data because it is coming so fast that the software needs to keep them in order. Different priorities might go on different queues.

A stored procedure is a routine that a programmer loads into the database. One such routine is what database companies call "triggers." These routines will look at the data going into rows and columns and cause something else to happen. An example could be the number of hats in an inventory program. When the number of hats goes below 10, a flag is triggered to order more hats.

The layout or schema of a database is set up before the database can be used. The index columns are also configured for speed. When the main software has completed its testing, the database will need to be cleared of all the test data. The empty database should have a loading data test. There could be a special order in which the data must be entered. The database is now ready to be populated with the customer's data. Questions to ask:

system engineer		Do you use a database?
system engineer		Is it custom or commercial?
system engineer		Who controls the reads and writes to the database?
system engineer		Who wrote the software?
system engineer		Are there any stored procedures in the database?
system engineer		Are there any triggers in the database?
system engineer		Are they documented?
system engineer		Have they been tested with live data?
system engineer		How are the stored procedures and triggers tested?
system engineer		What are the trigger points?
system engineer		What does the trigger do when fired?

It is the responsibility of the main software group to test all of this database software to prove that it works the way that the supplier stated. Nothing should be taken for granted.

16.1.3 Package Software

To save money and time, it is sometimes cost effective to buy an outside software package. These could be:

- Databases
- Networks
- Internet connections
- Communication packages
- Report writers
- Statistic packages

There are more specialized packages. If the package has been used by the main software team for a long time, it would receive a pass on the questions. But if they have been using the package for years and they are on a new release from the supplier, they need in-house testing with the main software to confirm that no modifications are needed.

General packages such as communication, report writers, and statistical packages can use these questions:

system engineer		Are you using any outside packages?
system engineer		Do you have the tech documents for your programmers?
system engineer		Are you using the package as designed?
system engineer		(No) what are you doing differently? (follow the trail)
system engineer		What revision are you using?
system engineer		What is the date to be implemented?
system engineer		Do you receive updated modules (service packs) for this revision?
system engineer		Are you up to date with the package?
system engineer		Do you receive updates automatically?
system engineer		How does the licensing work?
system engineer		Does the company pay for each user's installation?

The database itself does not come with the interface or stored procedure routines shown above. The setup and administrative parts can slow down a development team. Here are the database questions:

system engineer		Who is the database administrator?
system engineer		How were they trained?
system engineer		Is the database in one server?
system engineer		What is the database package name?
system engineer		What revision is the database and date you received it?
system engineer		Is it password protected?
system engineer		If the database is moved to a new server, how do you modify the program?
system engineer		Does the program use a password to get to the database or the individual files?

Networks have become pretty well standardized. But you still have a few questions:

system engineer		Is the system connected to the company network?
system engineer		How do you stop personnel from other departments from getting to the data?
system engineer		Can the network handle the volume of data you need to transmit?
system engineer		If the messages cannot get through, is there a queuing routine?

Internet questions can be a book in themselves, so I'll stick to the basics:

system engineer		What kind of firewall do you have?

system engineer		Can employees get to all files from the Internet?
system engineer		What security are you doing above the firewall? (general details)
system engineer		What is your backup if your connection goes down?

16.1.4 Protocols for Specialized Hardware

The protocol is the sequence used to communicate to a hardware unit. An example of this is the computer in a car. The computer requests status from the engine and, with that status, the computer controls gas flow. This handshaking might require many messages between the modules. Questions to ask:

system engineer		Does the system have any special hardware?
system engineer		Did the main software group write the software to control it?
system engineer		Do you have a document showing the acceptable messages?
system engineer		(Yes) May I see it? (Document name, and so on)
system engineer		Do you have a design plan?
system engineer		(Yes) May I see it? (Document name, and so on)
system engineer		Do you have a test plan?
system engineer		Has the test been run?
system engineer		(Yes) Show me the results.

16.1.5 Operating Systems

Basically there are three major areas to watch for and understand.

First, is the operating system the right one for this product? You need to know if the operating system can handle what the software needs. If the system is writing 50 records per second to the database, there is no problem, but if there are 50,000 records, can the system handle it? With the X size of the system, can a request for information be returned in N seconds? Sometimes it is a matter of someone doing the math to see whether the operating system can handle the throughput. Do not forget to include a growth factor. The questions for this are in Chapter 21 in the performance section.

> Last Christmas one of the big electronics stores' cash register system was so slow that the cashier and I had time to talk about the DVD I had picked up. I asked him why a sales person said that he could not check inventory for an item I wanted. He said that they were told not to use it because it slowed the system even more.

Second, find out if the system is the latest system. If the project is near the end or behind schedule, it would be a roll of the dice to put in a new operating system. Question the statement that it is a drop-in operating system that will not have any effect. Some companies have lost months reworking their software to be compatible with the newest operating system. To reduce the risk, let other companies do the initial debugging. Sometimes, companies need something new that will only be available in the next generation operating system. If the company has a new operating system, you should mark it as a risk. The first question below could be a multipart question. There could be different parts that use different operating systems (for example, individual PCs, and different servers):

system engineer		What operating system do you use?
system engineer		How long have you been using it?

Third, does this have to work on a number of PC systems? Everyone has seen "This software will run on Microsoft Windows Vista, XP, 2000, 98, and 95." The company's list of operating systems has to be tested with the software product:

system engineer		Does your product run on a PC?
system engineer		Have all operating systems been tested with your product?

system engineer		What operating systems will it work on?
system engineer		What operating system does the control (or admin) console run on?
system engineer		What is the recommended screen resolution for the product?
system engineer		Do you test the other resolutions?

16.2 INDIRECT SOFTWARE

Now we can look at the software that is not included in the product, but still has an impact on the development. Basically, this software is supporting the development of the product.

Examples of this software would be:

- Homegrown debug software

- Simulation software/test equipment

- Automated software testing scripts

- Installation scripts

- Software to populate a database

Any indirect software that is used during development could affect the final product. If the software they are counting on to help them has its own bug, the programmers could chase a problem for days just to find out the support software had the bug. These programs need to be tested as much as the main software.

See Chapter 11 for development tools.

16.2.1 Homegrown Debugging Software

During development, a programmer could write a special routine to help him debug his software. The programmer is responsible for the data and methods used. If it does not work correctly, it is the programmer's problem.

Some companies find that a debug program written by one of their own programmers becomes a common tool. The next programmer will add a piece to it and it grows. This becomes a major in-house tool. If programmer "A" writes the code and programmer "B" uses it, programmer "B" could be working on a program that looks good with the tool, but the tool could have a bug that masks the problem.

This type of program grows on the demand of the programmer. It is a true write-as-you-go thing. This is probably the only place you do not need a software development plan, but someone independent of the writer must test it. Questions:

programmer		Do you use any homegrown debugging tools?
programmer		Who tested it (them) for accuracy?
programmer		How do you control changes to the program?
programmer		Does it have a version number or letter?
programmer		Is it under version control?
programmer		Is there a known problem in the program?
programmer		When the debug tool starts, does it show the version number?

16.2.2 Simulation Software/Test Equipment

The company is developing a system that will simulate a 30-story elevator control. It's unlikely the developer would have an elevator 30 stories high, so a piece of test equipment would be built. The point is that this simulation might be written by another group or even the software team itself. This whole approach brings up many questions:

programmer		Does development use a simulation program?
programmer		Does development use test equipment?
programmer		Does it have software?
		(Yes) Who wrote it?
		Development plan?
		Software specification?
		Test plan?
		Test results?
		Version controlled?
		Are the changes controlled by the software board?
		How is the program loaded?
		How do you know it is the latest software?
		Was the software peer reviewed?

16.2.3 Automated Software Testing Scripts

Many companies use automated testing programs. Usually you start by recording the keystrokes used to step through the program. Next, the script is modified for testing more paths through the software. These scripts are written by specialists, but they might be part of development, testing, or quality. There is a section about automated software test scripts in Chapter 21. Questions to ask:

programmer		Do you use automated software testing?
programmer		Package, homegrown, or mixed?
programmer		(Yes) Who writes the scripts?
	·	Development plan?
		Software specification?
		Test plan?
		Test results?
		Script peer reviewed?

16.2.4 Installation Scripts

A few companies created Installation packages that are used to install their product into PCs and servers. Although these packages are simple to use, the results of the install must be checked. The configuration after the install must also be checked. The programs allow the operator to choose options during the installation, and the operator has to know all the options work. Questions to ask:

programmer		Is an installation program used?
programmer		(Yes) Is there an installation plan that includes configuration?
programmer		Test plan?
programmer		Test results?
programmer		Configuration controlled?
programmer		Are there version numbers or letters?
programmer		How are changes controlled?
programmer		Do the installation version numbers or letters appear?
programmer		Does the installation program show the main software version?

16.2.5 Software to Populate a Database

The programmer needs a fresh database to test a report program. The programmer may work on a problem for weeks before he looks at the database for errors. Spreadsheet programs are used to create an export data file to be used as an import into the database. Some problems you might encounter: The column might be off between the spreadsheet and the receiving database, or the data in the column might just be wrong. Questions to ask:

programmer		Is there a script to load the database?
programmer		Was the data reviewed before being used to create the database?
programmer		Who reviewed the data once it was installed in the database?

16.3 SUMMARY

The main take-away from this chapter is simple. When you find software outside the main development plan, a set of questions must be asked:

programmer		Who wrote it?
programmer		Was there a plan?
programmer		Software development plan?
programmer		Was there peer review on the code?
programmer		Is there a test plan?
programmer		Where are the results?
programmer		Is the software under configuration control?
programmer		How do you track bugs or incidents?

17

Firmware

To understand what firmware is, let's look at some definitions:

- If you search for "firmware" on the Internet, it comes up on Wikipedia as, "Firmware is a computer program that is embedded in a hardware device"—"As its name suggests, firmware is somewhere between hardware and software. Like software, it is a computer program which is executed by a computer."[1]

- "An intermediate form between hardware and software is firmware, which consists of software embedded in electronic devices during their manufacture."[2]

Firmware is executable code running a processor. The executable code is built by running a software language program through a compiler. It can be written by engineers or programmers. There should be rules to govern the development of the firmware. If the auditee resists discussing it, write it as a risk for management to deal with. Report this risk during the daily review or directly to the escort. The auditee might have it resolved by the next day.

More and more firmware is appearing on circuit boards, replacing complex circuits. Firmware could be part of a project or the whole project, so you need to take a close look at the processes.

To find out if there is firmware in the project, ask if the company is selling circuit boards with the system. If they do, ask to see each board or drawing. Ask the engineer which chip is the processor. If they point out a processor, there is firmware.

---

[1]From Wikipedia.org. Accessed November 26, 2007.
[2]Andrew S. Tanenbaum (1990). *Structured Computer Organization,* 3rd ed. (Englewood Cliffs, NJ: Prentice Hall).

As an auditor you will find there are no standards that state what is to be done with firmware development. Treat firmware as software because the main functions are the same:

- Version control

- Change control

- Planning

- Testing

- Integration

Additional functions need to be audited: handling of firmware, part numbering, and manufacturing controls, which will be reviewed later in this chapter.

Here is the point to watch out for: The functions for software and firmware are the same but the processes might be different. A company can force firmware to follow the software processes and thereby could double the cost of development. Again, it makes common sense to audit their process. Do not let the auditee tell you that it has always been done this way. You are doing an audit to find development risks and cost problems.

Use the questions from the configuration control, test, and integration sections. Most of these questions would be the same; any differences will be listed later:

- Planning   • Part of testing

- Design   • Configuration control (not version control)

17.1 PLANNING

The firmware development plan would show the schedule and budget for the circuit card. The firmware part in the plan might be minimal and mixed in with a few boilerplate statements. It might be part of the total product plan or it might be glossed over. Without having defined, specialized standards there is nothing to hold it to, so it's frequently passed over.

If the project is a series of boards or just one board, inputs and outputs must be defined. What is the format of the communications and what are the expected outputs? Questions to ask:

	1	Does your project use firmware?
	2	Was a plan developed for the firmware?
	3	Will you be using chip sets?

	4	Will you be designing the circuits that the firmware will control?
	5	What processor will the firmware use?
	6	How will you store the firmware code? (Flash, ROM, EEROM)
	7	Has the plan been peer reviewed?
	8	May I see the minutes of the meeting?
	9	Review the minutes. Were hardware and software people there?

17.2 DESIGN

The design of the product will show what each circuit board will be required to perform. A list of all the signals, circuits, and functions will be laid out. The planning is different than software because the firmware is designed during the board design.

The electrical engineer will design the board from the specification, and the engineer will decide what circuits need to be controlled by firmware. The selection of the right processor can be delayed until more of the specifications are refined. Size and speed are the two main attributes the engineer considers. Smaller and slower processors generally are less expensive.

Sometimes a designer will use a chip set to perform a function on the board. A chip set is a group of chips that the manufacturer combines to perform a specific task. For example, a chip set could be for an Ethernet communication port. The manufacturer designs this to sell their products and save their customers time in designing and testing.

As the auditor you should review any design documentation that is available. Here are a few questions:

	1	Has the design been peer reviewed? By whom?
	2	Is the design document clear?
	3	Are there any unknown details or missing parts?
	4	What processor will be used?
	5	Why that processor?

17.3 TESTING

Testing of firmware must be precise. When something is input into the firmware, the results are exact and known, so a detailed test plan is a must. Each requirement must have a test point to prove the requirement works. There is a direct correlation between each test and each requirement. All conditions should be listed, with the known inputs matched with the corresponding outputs. The tester will need to be able to see what lines are high or low. Low is no voltage and high is voltage, so special equipment or a scope might be needed. You are looking for the test plan with step-by-step instructions and known results. Questions to ask:

	1	Is there a test plan?
		Is the test plan document under configuration control?
	2	Has the test plan been peer reviewed? By whom?
	3	Is there a space on each line to be checked off after the step is completed?
	4	After a problem has been fixed, is the test started from the beginning?
	5	Is the final test run by someone other than the designer/programmer?
	6	How is the firmware proven to be the correct version? (checksum?)
	7	Is the firmware retested if circuits are changed?
	8	Are the values from A/D conversions checked?
	9	Are the results of the testing documented?
	10	Where are the results stored?
	11	May I please see some results?
	12	Is the name of the tester on the sheet?
	13	Is the version of firmware shown?
	14	Are the date, time, test number, and location listed?
	15	Are the results clear?
	16	Do results show pass or fail with notes?
	17	How are failures tracked?

17.4 CONFIGURATION CONTROL

Configuration control has two levels in the firmware world. The first is the standard storing of the firmware code in a configuration control system, which may be used to build a version of the firmware. The test plans and the test results should also be linked to the version and controlled.

The second is which version of the firmware works with which version of the hardware. If a chip or a circuit is changed, the configuration of the board and the firmware must be retested with the original test plan. Questions to ask:

	1	If the board is changed, what happens to the part number?
	2	Does the part number reflect the firmware version?
	3	If the firmware changes, does the part number change?
	4	If the firmware changes, does a dash number change?

17.5 PRODUCTION

Most companies that work with circuit boards have drawings showing the layout of the components. The firmware version number should be on the drawing. This shows that this firmware works with this board.

In most companies, this section could be skipped. But if the firmware is being changed frequently, it is an important section. This is the only time this book will go into manufacturing. If manufacturing sends out circuit boards with the wrong firmware, it will cost the company in dollars and customer satisfaction.

> A few years ago, a company sent out hundreds of new circuit boards for a new release of their product. The board was less expensive and faster. It was a major marketing event for the company. Within a week, they were getting calls for support. The boards were not working. The entire lab testing before the release showed the board working perfectly. The firmware that was loaded on the board was one version older than the product release version. This mistake hurt the company. Every board had to be shipped back to the company, repaired, and sent back to the customer—all at the company's expense.

How the firmware gets from development to the product floor is paramount in the release process. Question every word used to describe how they move it to the production floor. Watch for remarks like "Oh, the operator downloads the firmware from the network." Go after what the choices are on the network. If it is a bank of all of the developed firmware, how does the operator know which to take? And if there is a new release, how would the operator know about it? The new modern way to do business is the company network. If there is only one firmware version in the directory where the operator looks for it, there would be no way of picking the wrong firmware.

Now go after the circuit boards themselves. How do they load the firmware onto the boards? Do they load a chip (ROM) or flash memory then add it to the board, or do they load the firmware directly into the board? Now how do they confirm that the firmware was loaded correctly? Are they using a checksum? A checksum is a formula that simply adds the machine code and comes up with a number. This number is unique for this firmware. If the checksums from development match the board, they are the same. Another option is to compare what they load to what is in the product after it has been loaded. Both ways work. They need to do something to check that the board was loaded correctly.

When someone hands you a board, how do you know what version of firmware is on that board? There are many ways to show this information:

	1	How does the firmware release get from development to manufacturing?
	2	What is the procedure or the way you release firmware?
	3	Where does manufacturing get the release?
	4	Does the operator load the firmware from the network?
	5	Is there more than one firmware file at that location?
	6	How is the firmware loaded onto the board?
	7	How does manufacturing confirm that the firmware was loaded correctly?
	8	Is any equipment used to check out the whole board?
	9	How does manufacturing receive new releases?
	10	Looking at the board, how do you know the firmware version?
	11	Is the firmware loaded into a chip or flash memory?

	12	Does the chip or flash have a part number?
	13	How are the chips or flash handled?
	14	How many bad chips or flash do you receive from your supplier?

More and more companies are now using equipment that checks the entire board. This equipment checks the circuits and sees how the firmware works with the board. If the auditee uses this testing equipment, ask about the configuration and testing of its software.

18

Software Coding Standards

What is a coding standard? It is the format and rules by which a programmer writes and documents his code. Does one standard work for all languages? No, some languages document better than others. Each language will have its own standard and a project could be written in more than one language. The monitor portion might be in Visual Basic, C++ might be used internally, and a report writer might be used to generate reports.

Why should a programmer use a coding standard? Let's answer this with another question. What happens if a programmer leaves the company? With everyone developing to the coding standard, there would be minimal impact on the project. In a short period of time, the new programmer would be up to speed making changes or making corrections.

Programming standards can be particularly valuable to a large organization producing software. The language can be used in an undisciplined style to develop programs unreadable to all except the original programmer. Even the original programmer might not remember enough after a period of time. The uniformity will make the maintenance job much easier and save the company a major rewrite expense.

ISO/IEC 14882 Programming Language C++ Standard is a huge piece of work (over 700 pages) that contains all that anyone needs to know if working in C++. However, because of its size, many companies will write their own abridged version of it or some other programming standard in creating their coding standard. These usually end up being 25 to 150 pages and a lot more manageable. As an auditor, you are not going to learn their programs. You will not be checking syntax (the layout of the code) or finding logic errors. You will be looking at the documentation within the program.

The things that need auditing are:

- Program headers

- Routine headers

- Naming conventions

- Data structures

- Data definitions

> As a young programmer, I was given a software package that had been developed for an oil distributor. My job was to figure out how it worked because the original programmer had left the company. There was no documentation of any kind. It took me six weeks to understand how the programmer laid out the files and what was the input and the output. The company was then able to demo it to a potential customer with enough confidence that if it were sold, I could customize the program.

> Years later, I was one of five consultants working for a large company with a new product line. We were brought on board to jump-start the project. We had been contracted to get it up and running for the company's computer group to take over. One night at dinner, a fellow consultant told me that they would never be able to let him go, because the software he wrote was so complex. It was built on tables pointed to other tables that pointed to another table. He said it would take them too long to figure out how it was done and there was no documentation. When the project was handed over, the company was basically forced into hiring that consultant. This is an unethical way to achieve job security and breaches the inherent consultant/company understanding.
>
> This is not an uncommon story.

I can easily add another 100 examples of why programmers need to document. Here are the three biggest reasons it is not being done: bartering for a job, job security, and the programmer doesn't have the time.

Ask the programming manager for a list of programs with the programmers' names. Pick one program per name and ask for a printout of that program. If there is any documentation for the program, you will need that as well. You might have to reassure them that they can have it back before you leave the department. Find a quiet place and get a feel for how they documented the software.

Today more and more companies are using packages that analyze the programs. These packages are improving with every version. If the project is using one of these packages, review the findings. Ask questions about the results.

Step by step instructions to review the coding documentation are included in the next section.

18.1 PROGRAMS AND THE DOCUMENTATION

First, did you get the program you asked for or were you given a different program? Since you selected, you got a random sample. There should be enough documentation so that someone else could step in to make changes or make updates. You do not need to be a programmer to do this. See if the documentation is clear on what will be in the program. Does the documentation show all of the functions? Can you match the functions to the routine performing it? Have there been code reviews? Look at the minutes and findings for the reviews.

Do not worry about the syntax of the code—the compiler will check that. If you want a close look at the code, bring in a programmer from outside the project. It is a toss of the coin to take someone from within the company you are auditing. On the one hand, they know the rules for the code and, on the other, it is their coworker. Questioning the guest programmer's findings and picking a couple of areas will give you a feel for the code.

Documentation in a program is like a tour map. It leads you through the code and points out everything of interest. It explains with details the history, formulas, special areas, and choice of paths. When you are finished, you should now be able to trace through the logic.

18.2 PROGRAM HEADERS

The first page of the program is the header page. This provides the general information about the whole program. Here is a basic list with some details of what is needed:

- Name of the company

- Copyright information

- Restrictions on the program—company secret, disposal requirements, proprietary notice

- Name of the program

- Description or summary of the program or function(s)

- List of the programs that call this program

- Entry criteria—definition of any data passed to this program
- List of what programs or routines this program calls
- Special set-up information with descriptions
- History block with:
  - Date that includes the original release and updates
  - Version numbers or letters
  - Description of the change(s)
  - Programmer's name
  - Review numbers or dates (if there are peer reviews)
  - Testers' names

		Is the company name shown?
		Is there a copyright statement?
		Is the program's name shown?
		Is there a summary/purpose description for this program?
		Is there a history block?
		Is the original release date shown?
		Does the history block have a date and revision numbers/letters?
		Does the history block have the programmer's name?
		Does the history block have a summary of the changes?
		Are the testers' names listed?
		Are there definitions of the inputs for this program?
		Are there definitions of the outputs?
		Is there an initialization routine to set up the program?
		Are the global variables defined first, or are they in a master program?
		Are variables in groups? Explain?

This box of questions is used for each program. I can't emphasize enough that this is a business risk that must be evaluated. None of these is required, but it makes good common sense to check to see what is being completed. There should be no confusion about the program when you look at that first page. The absence of the programmer's name on the first page of the program means the programmer is counting on the file name that the programmer created. What happens if someone copies the program and it is renamed?

18.3 BODY OF THE PROGRAM

At the beginning of each routine, there should be information about that routine. Here is the basic information needed (with some details):

- Name of the routine.

- Summary description.

- List of the entry points (if more than one).

- What data is needed and what is the format (integer, byte)?

- What is the output and what is the format?

- History of changes (optional).

- What happens when an error occurs?

- Explain decision points and paths to take.

		Does the module's name make sense?
		Is there a summary description?
		Does each subroutine have a defined input?
		Does each subroutine have a defined output?
		Is there more than one exit point in the routine?
		Is there an error-handling routine?
		Is error information sent to a system/program log?
		Are there notes in the routine that are useful for testing/reviews?
		Do the lines of code have comments that are clear?
		Are formulas or algorithms explained or referenced somewhere?

		Are the decision options explained?
		Is the variable well defined and clearly labeled?

18.4 NAMING CONVENTIONS

If all programmers made up their own names for routines or variables, how would another programmer looking at the code know what it is? Type names are identifiers that are not a function of data. These include:

- Names of classes

- Unions

- Structures

The auditor needs to research the naming conventions the auditee is using and where is it is documented. This is usually an identifier, which is a set of one to four characters with an underscore and the name. Capitals and lower case can be used whichever way the auditee would like. You will also see names of variables dealing with numbers defining the type of number such as integer or floating. If there are no naming conventions, the project could still work, but the cost of changes for upgrades and code fixes skyrockets. Questions to ask:

		Are naming conventions in place?
		Please show me the definitions or documentation for it.
		Have global names been defined?
		Are the number fields defined?
		Is everyone using the same naming convention?
		Has a programmer explained all of the names?

> I reviewed a program years ago, and the routine created the header for a message packet. This programmer had a sense of humor and named the routines for parts of a head. The program used mouth, ear, nose, and eye routines. You never know what you will see in the code.

18.5 STRUCTURES

A database is made up of different files, all related. Each file has records, which are made up of fields. The fields are pieces of data that must be defined. All fields are related to the record.

A message used to communicate is also divided into fields. The order of the fields in the message and the definitions of the fields must be defined.

The physical view structure is another way of referring to the fields in a record or message. Somewhere in the system there must be a definition of the structures used in the database or messages. This is sometimes called a data dictionary or defined structures. Questions to ask:

		Is there a database in the system?
		Are all the files defined?
		Are all the records within the files defined?
		Are any messages defined?
		Where is the definition of the structures or schemas?
		May I see them?
		Is the structure name clear about the data it holds?
		Are data ranges defined?
		Is each field clear about the data it will hold?
		Are any limits set on fields?
		Does it give you the size of the field?
		Are any fields defined as indexed?
		Does the index state whether the field cannot be duplicated?
		Are any stored procedures used in the database?
		Show me the documentation for the stored procedures.
		Are these procedures defined somewhere?
		Who handles the programming of stored procedures?

See if you can take some of the database information and track it back to a document and design specification. Check to see if the document matches and whether updates were made to the documents. Many programmers might be using the database, and without definitions, everyone can use the fields differently.

18.6 AUTO-GENERATED CODE

Are the programmers using an auto-generated code package to build their code? This works on simple routines or starting up routines. Auto-generated or code generators are becoming more prevalent in large software projects. The setting up of classes in C++ is one of the most common uses.

With development models, there are packages that will generate code automatically. These packages also can regenerate code when a model is updated.

Here are a few shortcomings in code generation:

- Code generators are black boxes—what you get is what you get. You cannot go into the generator to make it do things differently.

- Buggy—they are getting better, but they do have bugs. There might be bugs for areas rarely used.

- Code can be hard to understand and review.

- Sometimes a requirement might be missed due to different types of data (an unusual requirement).

Review how these auto-generated routines stand up against verification and validation testing. Look closely at the test plan to see how the auditee will test these routines.

19

Metrics

In software, we use metrics as a method of measurement in a comparative sense. Metrics can be great. They can tell you where the company has been and how much progress it has made. For example, let's say a company report says software has a quality cost on average of $15,000 per month. Management wants this number dropped to below $5000 per month. Each month the department tries different things to lower the rework expenses. If the amount goes up, the change made it worse, and the company backs out of the change. If the amount goes down, the company is moving in the right direction. The metric here is the measurable comparison between the average ($15,000 per month) and the new monthly figure.

Metrics can also be numbers that have no useful meaning if the data used to develop the metric is incorrect or skewed. Skewing can happen when two pieces of data that are related but independent are mixed together. A good example of this is corrective action requests for documents and software bugs. They are both corrective actions but added together they mean nothing. Together they give you the total number of problems for the project, but you cannot use them to see what is needed to improve the development.

During your audit, you should be asking about the metrics that are used to measure the production and effectiveness of the department. When you are shown a metric of any kind, question where it comes from, what creates the numbers and how does it help the department. The incident analysis grid metric covered in Chapter 11 is one of the best measurements. It focuses attention on areas in development that need improvement. I worked with a company that used the grid. In reviewing the grid, we discovered that most incidents occurred during the hand-off from design to programming. When we changed the format of the data being passed from one group to the other, the incident number decreased dramatically. The biggest thing with this metric is that it is under utilized and/or not used correctly. Good metric, poor follow-through.

One of the worst metrics is how many anomalies (incidents) there are or how many anomalies occur per thousand lines of code each programmer creates. It's not a good measurement because it provides a skewed metric response. To illustrate: Imagine comparing an entry-level programmer's lines of code to that of a highly skilled programmer working on an advanced system with a high degree of difficulty. By that standard, the entry-level worker will look like the better producer.

Metrics are hit and miss. The metrics from one company will not work at another. Think of applying metrics to a song writer. How many lines were written today? Programmers are writing code, and how fast they write means nothing if it does not work.

Here is a comment written in the ASQ journal *Software Quality Professional:* "The firm's efforts to implement software quality metrics were meant mainly to fulfill management and planning objectives."[1]

Occasionally, you will run across totally meaningless metrics. These tend to occur when a company attempts to keep up with a newly emerging industry standard or to fulfill a management mandate. What you end up with is likely to be the creation of charts and graphs to match what already is known. This will have no effect on the project because there are no real findings.

Mark Baker, in "Implementing an Initial Software Metrics Program," states: "Software is invisible and seemly intangible, but that does not mean that we cannot provide quantitative basis for making decisions."[2]

Baker has some excellent guidelines: "Through the study and proven experience of the past years, several factors that seriously influence the success of a metrics program have come to light. They are as follows:

1. Select measures that respond to the needs of the organization.

2. Chose measures that are unobtrusive to the organization's development activities.

3. Know what to expect from these measures.

4. Convince management that measurement is necessary."[3]

Once you have a metric program in place, it's not foolproof. Watch for human interpretation of the data and the places where data can be moved. Interpretation

---

[1]Daniel Galin, "Software Quality Metrics—From Theory to Implementation," *ASQ Software Quality Professional,* vol. 5, issue 3 (June 2003), 25.
[2]Mark D. Baker, "Implementing an Initial Software Metrics Program," CH3007-2/91/0000-1289 IEEE.
[3]Mark D. Baker, "Implementing an Initial Software Metrics Program," CH3007-2/91/0000-1291 IEEE.

depends on point of view, experience with the metric, and even personal integrity (does a particular interpretation benefit an individual or group?). Moving the data has risk because it can be manipulated and results will be skewed.

When management asks for a quantitative measurement, the numbers they receive will change in a positive way. "If it is tracked, the numbers will get better" (Hawthorne Effect). There are many reasons (some positive, some negative) why this occurs. When all attention is focused on an area with your numbers, two things can happen:

(1) A concerted effort to improve the output with focus shifting to better their numbers. On the other hand, a desire to be out of the scrutiny of management could lead to. . .

(2) Improving the numbers reported to management without real measurable change having taken place.

If you are auditing metrics, here are some questions with a general application:

		Do you use metrics?
		What metrics do you use?
		What is the objective?
		What kind of metrics? (show me)
		What does this metric tell me?
		Where is the data used and where does it come from?
		Can I see the input data to the metric?
		Does this metric help?
		Show me how it helped.

19.1 AGING AND PRIORITY METRICS

The configuration chapter showed that all problems that software developers find should be put into a database or tracked somehow. Metrics are one way to put a numerical value on items to improve prioritizing. A good metric to use is the aging of open problems. "Aging a problem" means assigning it to 1 of 4 categories: Current, 30–60 days, 60–90 days, 90 days and over. As an auditor you should question each of the older open problems to determine the reason for the delay and why they weren't closed in a timely manner.

Using a priority status on each problem helps keep the project moving forward. The auditee must create a hierarchy of open problems. For example, 1—the program will not install or run, 2—a function does not work or gives false results, 3—the user cannot get into a function, and 4—a minor problem such as a misspelling or wrong color. Priorities 1, 2, or 3 should be handled before the lower level of problems. If any of these priorities remain open, the product is not ready to ship till they are closed.

19.2 PERFORMANCE METRICS

Why do we need performance metrics? If the new system/product cannot perform the tasks it is written to do, what good is it? It is the project team's job to monitor the performance. Program performance metrics are the best metric because they can be easily tracked. We need to measure performance against requirements. The numbers (outcome) should match or exceed the requirement. For example: if a program is required to store 10,000 records into the data in a second and testing shows it can only do 2,000, we have a usable metric. Now the programmer/designers know to make corrections to bring the performance to a point of meeting or exceeding the required 10,000 records.

You are auditing development. This can be a key element to the final product. If the development team does not check the performance of a system/product, they are not measuring performance against requirement. A whole system cannot be built on what a development team thinks the system can handle; they have to know.

Always ask, "What is the system required to do and what is the current tracked output?" Then question the answers given with, "How do you know?"

In Chapter 16, there is an example of a retail store that had people standing and waiting for a response from their system. The lines at each register grew by the second. Apparently, no one had ever checked the throughput of their system. The number of transactions should have been tracked until there was no delay in the response from the system and there should have been room for growth.

19.3 COMPLEXITY METRICS

To find out how complicated software is, designer/programmers use complexity metrics. Not all programs are equal. The firmware in the alarm clock does not have the same complexity as the software/firmware that is used in the space shuttle. Complexity metrics tell the user how much testing is needed to prove the program works.

Three areas need programs to work the first time and every time: military (including NASA and FAA), medical, and any program dealing with money. After all the bugs and incidents have been completed and cleared, the system should be tested from the beginning again (if possible by other testers). If anything is found and fixed, start from the beginning yet again until it makes it through the whole test without a failure.

The more complex the program, the more money should be spent on testing and integration, which may possibly exceed the cost of developing the software. As an auditor, you need to understand that if the software is complex and there is no room for doubt, the auditee should be doing extra steps in testing. There are program packages that will map the code usage areas to make sure each routine has been tested and reviewed.

NASA's independent verification and validation uses Halstead metrics. "Halstead complexity metrics were developed by the late Maurice Halstead as a means of determining a quantitative measure of complexity directly from the operators and operands in the module to measure a program module's complexity directly from source code."[4]

The complexity metric uses everything from how many blank lines exist to the number of decision points and how many levels down are the subroutines. There are white papers that use from 20 to 50 variables to compute the metric. Understand that these are serious calculations. Questions to ask:

		Is the software complex?
		Do you use a complexity metric?
		What formula do you use?
		Why do you use a complexity metric?
		How do you use the metric?

When you hear the company is using this type of metric, your first questions should be:

		How are you testing the product?
		How long is the test phase?
		Can you explain all the levels of the testing?

---

[4]Verifysoft Technology, "Measurement of Halstead Metrics with Testwell CMT++ and CMT Java." From http://www.verifysoft.com/en_halstead_metrics.html. Accessed May 17, 2008.

20

Independent Verification and Validation

Independent verification and validation (IV&V) is a series of technical and management activities performed by someone other than the developer of a system to improve the quality and reliability of that system and to ensure that the delivered product satisfies the user's operational needs.[1]

Software verification and validation (V&V) is a technical discipline of engineering. The purpose of software V&V is to help the development organization build quality into software during the software life cycle.[2]

The software department has a system to develop; the requirement specification list was put together at the start of the development process. Eventually the product is completed, delivered to the customer, and the software company expects payment. How do you know that all of the original requirements made it to the completed product? How much do you think a customer would be willing to pay for a system that started with 200 requirements and was delivered with only 184 requirements? The 184 requirements could be the best code ever delivered to a customer, but it would not mean a thing if the missing requirements were needed to run the customer's business or contained safety requirements.

To do the traceability would increase costs. No one wants to spend any extra to do a project. If the company is willing to do the traceability, it will pay off in customer satisfaction and save development costs from rewrites or adding missing requirements.

A standard that gives more information about IV&V is IEEE 1012 Standard for Software Verification and Validation.[3] This standard is 110 pages and a great resource.

---

[1] Robert O. Lewis, "Independent Verification & Validation: A Life Cycle," *Engineering Process for Quality Software,* Wiley Series in New Dimensions in Engineering 1992, 7.
[2] IEEE Std 1012 2004, Standard for Software Verification and Validation, 8 June 2005, iii.
[3] IEEE Std. 1012—2004 Standards for Software Verification and Validation.

In your audit, you must hit on this subject. How does software development know when a project has all the requirements included and it is complete? Even if the company you are auditing says they do not do traceability, you still need to understand how they know that everything is included in the final product. You will probably find some sort of tracking or checklist. Does everyone remember what was promised? Let's go back to the 200 requirements. How many people do you know who could remember 200 requirements word for word? Rewrites and redesign all can be traced back to requirements. This is a major area that drives up the cost of development.

Here are definitions for *verification* and *validation*.

- *Verification* is an iterative process aimed at determining whether the product of each step in the development cycle (a) fulfills all the requirements levied on it by the previous step and (b) is internally complete, consistent, and correct enough to support the next phase.

- *Validation* is the process of executing the software to exercise the hardware and comparing the test results to the required performance.[4]

A simple clarification comes from one of this book's peer reviewers (Donna Gregory):

- Verification is "was it done."

- Validation is "was it done right."

20.1 VERIFICATION

Verification is proving that all requirements can be traced through the system. You want to verify that all the requirements in the original specification make it all the way to the customer. This is a test completed not only at the end of the project, but also during each life-cycle phase. Using a traceability matrix, you can trace any requirement through a project to the acceptance testing. Let's create a sample traceability matrix. You start in the first document (which we have been calling the Functional Specification). It explains what is to be in the system. Number each requirement found in the Functional Specification (or first official document), using the acronym of the document and add a number (for example, FS1 for Functional Specification, Requirement 1). This is a simple form for the trace matrix. Your auditee can use their own system, as long as there is a system.

---

[4]Robert O. Lewis, "Independent Verification & Validation: A Life Cycle Engineering Process for Quality Software," Wiley Series in New Dimensions in Engineering 1992, 7.

Open a spreadsheet and put the word "Requirements" for a heading in column A. Put the first document "Functional Spec." as the header in column B. Put each document in the following columns. (See Figure 20.1) Type in a short description of the requirement into column A. Put the acronym/number into column B for the Functional Specification. Go through each document, finding the requirements, and add its acronym/number in the column under the document name (see Figure 20.1 Traceability Matrix).

You should be able to follow a requirement all the way to the acceptance test. This is a time-consuming process, but you should have all the columns filled in. If there are gaps, you need to look into the document for that requirement. In Figure 20.1 line 7 the requirement can be followed to Software Requirement and the column is blank. The probability of the requirement having been dropped is high. This is something you will need to investigate to see where the ball was dropped. If the test plans were written, then the Acceptance Test has been written from the functional specification, so the requirement will be tested. The missing requirement will be caught before the product leaves development. Hopefully a redesign to cover the missing requirement won't be necessary, but it does need to be in there.

Now let's look at the majority of the development departments, where the requirements are handed from one part of development to the next. As shown in Figure 20.1 line 4, this is the case where a design specification missed the requirement. By the time the product gets to acceptance testing, the requirement has been dropped until the customer reminds the developers. This problem is twofold. First, the programmer has to go back into the code and make the changes. Second, the customer may be dissatisfied and have doubts about the workmanship.

The worst time to lose a requirement is during the design phase of the project. Each requirement could change the approach used to fulfill the design.

The performance test column highlights the performance issues to be tested. These are the special tests that take extra time to prove or disprove.

Your job is to review a sampling of the traceability matrix. Understanding the process will get you get through the trace more easily. Many requirements are dropped when a big complex requirement takes up most of the developer's time. When the developer finishes that particular requirement, the schedule has tightened and the developer moves on to the next program. If the requirements are followed through the matrix, this does not happen.

Verification is performed at each phase of the development life cycle. Methods of verification include inspections, peer reviews, audits, walkthroughs, analyses, simulations, tests, and demonstrations.[5] The auditee must be able to present

---

[5]Mary Beth Chrissis, Mike Konrad, and Sandy Shrum, *CMMI Guidelines for Process Integration and Product Improvement* (Boston: Addison-Wesley), 576.

Traceability Matrix

A	B	C	D	E	F	G	H	I
Requirements	**Functional Spec.**	**System Requirements**	**Design Spec.**	**SW Requirements**	**Function Test Plan**	**Integration Test Plan**	**Performance Test Plan**	**Acceptance Test**
(1) No number fields will be blank	FS17	SR17	DS17	SW17	FT17	ITP17		AT17
(2) All buttons will be 1/2 in by 1 in.	FS18	SR18	DS18	SW18	FT18	ITP18		
(3) Inactive buttons will be disabled	FS23	SR23	DS23	SW23	FT23	ITP23		AT23
(4) User must re-login before running reports	FS34	SR34						
(5) Handle 200 store packets per minute	FS45	SR45	DS45	SW45	FT45	IPT45	PT45	PT45
(6) All prg auto log-out after 20 mins	FS64	SR64	DS64	SW64	FT64	ITP64	PT64	AT64
(7) During log-out all info will be saved	FS65	SR65	DS65			ITP65		AT65
(8) All screens will be in blues and white	FS05	SR05	DS05	SW05	FT05	ITP05		AT05

Figure 20.1   Traceability matrix.

proof that one or more of the above was completed before moving to the next life-cycle phase.

There is more about specifications in Chapter 14. Questons to ask:

manager		Do you have a traceability matrix?
manager		(Yes) May I have a copy of it? (Trace some requirements)
manager		(No) What do you do to trace requirements?
manager		How many requirements are in the functional specification?
review		Are the requirements clearly marked?
review		Ask two or more developers to explain a requirement
review		Are the requirements complete?
review		Are the requirements clear?
review		Are the requirements consistent?
review		Are the requirements testable?
review		Does the specification remain the same through each life cycle?
manager		Have the requirements been checked at each step in the life cycle?
manager		Who verifies that the requirements have been met?
manager		How many requirements are in the design specification?
manager		How many requirements are in the acceptance test?
tester		How many requirements are in the functional specification?
tester		How many requirements are in the design specification?
tester		How many requirements are in the acceptance test?
manager		Please tell me about a few of the requirements.

The reason for asking the number of requirements is a gross check through the system. If the numbers don't match, start looking into it.

20.2 VALIDATION

IEEE Std-1012 defines validation as (A) the process of evaluating a system or component during or at the end of the development process to determine whether it meets specified requirements. (B) The process of providing evidence that the software and its associated products satisfy system requirements allocated to software at the end of each life-cycle activity, solve the right problem, and satisfy intended use and user needs.[6]

During the development of a product, it is possible to confirm that requirements are completed within the product. Create a list of requirements in some common data area that shows who is responsible for the coding and unit testing of each requirement.

The testers can start looking at the requirements during the functional testing. The programs that contain a requirement can be checked off. The best place to check validation is during integration testing when the system is starting to come together. The tester should know which programs cover which requirements because the test was written from the design specification.

Now the development team is at the end of the project. The testers are running the acceptance tests without the customer. Everything looks like it's ready for the customer to come in and witness the final test for the signoff. Before development invites the customer, an independent (can be a tester if independent from programming) observer should sit with the tester to rerun the tests. The independent observer should check off each requirement when it has been witnessed and proven correct.

Here are some points to cover during validation auditing:

manager		Do you run validation tests?
manager		Do you have someone to validate the system?
manager		Were all the changes to the system documented?
manager		Do you run the validation test before the customer sees the system?
manager		How long does it take to run the validation test?
manager		How many performance requirements are there?
manager		Do you have the correct configuration for testing?
manager		Please show me the configuration you want in the system.

---

[6]IEEE Std. 1012–2004 Standards for Software Verification and Validation, 3.1.35–9.

manager		Please show me how you enter the configuration into the system.
auditor		Do the wanted and actual configurations match?
manager		Has the validation test been run on the correct configuration?
manager		Does the configuration change any of the requirements results?
manager		Does the acceptance test truly test each requirement?
manager		Is the tester starting from the beginning when an error occurs?
manager		Does a summary at the end of the acceptance test confirm the requirements?

You will notice that some of these questions are tied to other areas of the audit. Cross-checks help you perform a better audit and see how much the manager knows about the system. The questions about verification should all produce the same number of requirements. Answers to questions like "How long will the tests take?" reveal whether the person has even started thinking about the test.

Asking for test results will give you an idea if the requirements or the operational functions are being tested, using the number system from the traceability matrix. Look for references to requirements in the tests.

21

Testing

Testing is many things to many people; some see it as a major problem maker, others see it as a necessary part of development, and others as a cost saver. Testers are a good value because they usually do not get paid as much as a programmer (saving on cost) and it puts a second set of eyes on the program. However, with all the testing in the world, testing cannot build in quality. Testing can make a product with zero defects, but it cannot make it easy to operate, make colors that are pleasing to the eye, or produce a smooth flow of information.

Some companies do "gorilla" testing, which means people play with the product without a plan to see what they can break. It is not the best test that can be done; it will miss a large number of problems. A test plan is the best approach to cover the maximum area and hit the highest percentage of code. There is a place for "gorilla" testing, and some companies should add it to their tests. You never can predict what a customer is going to do when running a program. If there are buttons on a screen that have nothing to do with the function, push the buttons and see what happens. Users will hit any button on the screen at any time, usually some combination that a programmer never thought that a user would try. It is like my 89-year-old mother-in-law with a remote for her TV/VHS/DVD. She will hit any combination of buttons knowing that something will happen; she doesn't know what, but she hopes for the best.

There are two types of testing. The first is black box testing, when someone tests a program by entering known data and looking at the output. Think of a calculator: you enter 2, then plus, then 2 and the result key. The tester does not care what happens inside as long as 4 shows up as the result. Any other number would be a problem report. The second is white box testing, in which a tester will go into the code one step at a time to analyze and to scout for problems. White box testing is more expensive because the tester must have a higher skill level. In many cases, the white box tester will find the problem and bring the problem with the suggested fix to the programmer.

There are different levels of testing depending on where the software is in the development process. These levels are:

- Unit testing

- Function testing

- Integration testing

- Acceptance testing

- Regression testing

- Automated testing

- Performance testing

How does the test group figure out a time frame for their testing? It could take a week or the same amount of time as the development. If the development were perfect or close, the time would be short. If they had no idea what they were doing, it could take a long time.

When the schedule is made, testers are asked how long will they need to check out the whole project, if everything is perfect. What they really want to know is what is the minimum testing time. For example, let's say the project starts January 1 and testers will get the module to be tested on July 1, with the delivery of final product August 1. In May the development team sees that it will take an extra week to complete the project. We know the customer wants it on August 1, so the test time starts to shrink. By July 1, there is a two-week overrun; testing just lost another week. Having been a quality director for several companies, I've managed test teams as part of quality. Sadly, this is not the exception but the norm. If this were my project, I would be looking for extra time for two reasons: First, it is going to take a month to check out the product, and just because the time is cut doesn't mean that the code will have fewer errors. Second, when a team is under pressure to get it done, shortcuts and mistakes happen. Quality in the second delivery does not help the company's image when the first delivery didn't work.

Estimating the test time is not easy. How do testers know how many problems will surface during testing? If they are putting a man on the moon or making a device that monitors a patient in the hospital, there is no room for error in the final code. Some companies have a small test budget so they fix any open problems they encounter—they don't look for work. The balance is how much time does the company allow for testing and how many errors is it willing to send to the field.

How much testing is performed is a management decision. The more time the testing group has to test, the deeper the testing can go into the product. If it is

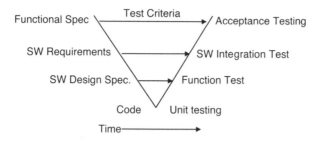

Figure 21.1   Correlations between specifications and testing.[1]

done right from the beginning and a good set of regression tests are developed, the time might be shortened.

Here is the relationship between the specifications and the test documents that should be developed. When you look at Figure 21.1, you will see the functional specification. As you know, the first document developed by software is the functional specification. When it is completed, the test department should receive a copy of it to develop the acceptance test. Going down the left side of the "V", you see the software requirements and across you will see the integration testing. The next level down is software design specification with the process or function testing. The lowest level is the coding with unit testing.

Once the code with the unit testing is finished, the tester will use the function test plan to test. This is continued up the right side of the "V." All the names that could be used for both sides of the "V" depend on the company you are auditing.

You also need to be aware that testing uses the development budget and problems fixed in the field, use the field service budget. The simple point is that they all look at it from their functional costs. As the auditor, you need to look at it from the total cost to the company. Development might let a minor error get out in the field and let field service fix it, so it comes from their budget. Notice in Figure 21.2 (which is also in Chapter 15) that, depending on how many products are in the field, every dollar saved in development could cost hundreds in the maintenance area. Some products might need to be sent back to manufacturing to be reprogrammed. I have seen a company spend more money on shipping products back and forth than the units' retail price.

In each area there should be test plans—how detailed is management's call, but if any group is missing a plan, it becomes a risk factor.

---

[1]Robert O. Lewis, "Independent Verification & Validation: A Life Cycle Engineering Process for Quality Software," *Wiley Series in New Dimensions in Engineering,* 37. (Simplified for this discussion.)

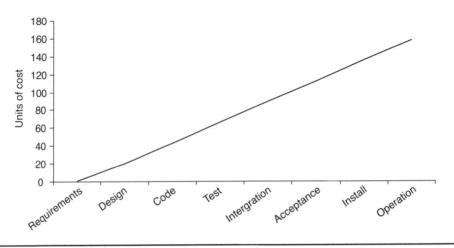

Figure 21.2   Cost of an error over the software life cycle.[2]

Different test equipment will affect the software project, so there is a test equipment section in this chapter.

21.1 UNIT TESTING

Unit testing is usually done by individual programmers on their own work. Sometimes other independent testers will perform the unit test. To make sure that it works the way they believe it should, sometimes a tester will help a programmer write some unit tests. Two factors here are whether the tester is available and whether the programmer asks for help. Cooperation is a sign of a good relationship between programmers and testers. Questions to ask:

programmer		Do you perform unit testing?
programmer		Does anyone perform unit testing?
programmer		Do you plan the unit testing?
programmer		Do you prepare the results on paper before trying the testing?
programmer		How do you confirm the results?
programmer		Do you sit down with the tester before giving them your software for testing?

---

[2]John W. Horch, *Practical Guide to Software Quality Management* (Boston: Artech House 1996), 48.

programmer		How do you give the tester your software?
programmer		Do you get along with the tester(s)?

Inexperienced programmers have a hard time with unit testing. They do not realize the extent of the testing they need to perform because they do not see the bigger picture:

programmer		How long have you been programming?
programmer		Do you like debugging routines?
programmer		Can you show me a unit test sheet or plan?

You do not need a formal unit test plan. What you want to see is that they put some thought into the testing before it was run.

21.2 FUNCTIONAL TESTING

This level of testing confirms that the modules are working as designed. The most important part of these tests is to prove that the software works as planned. The plan should be a one-for-one design specification to the functional test point. This reinforces that the design specification must be reviewed by the testers to make sure that specification points are testable. Do not allow the testers to tell you that they use the software design document as the test plan. If they are interpreting the document, they never do it the same way twice. Each time say they can start in the middle, start questioning—it must always be started at the beginning. Test departments do a quick turnaround in quality when they start writing the plans. I worked with a vice president who did not want to waste money on the plans. After the plans were developed and proven to have reduced errors and cost, the vice president wanted a copy of the plans to show corporate, who came to visit because of the turnaround in quality.

One of the biggest points to understand is that if a test fails, the tester must be able to run the test a second time and come up with the exact same error. This way, when the tester gives the error to the programmer, the programmer will be able to duplicate the error. All the steps leading up to the error must be recorded. (See Chapter 11 on configuration control.) Questions to ask:

programmer		Do you perform function testing?
tester		Do you have a documented plan for function testing?

tester		(Yes) Is the plan document under configuration control?
tester		(No) How do you know you covered the whole function test?
tester		Do you have the setup instructions documented for the function testing?
tester		Will you reuse the function test plan on other products?
tester		Is the setup instruction under configuration control?
tester		How do you track the time used to run each test?
tester		Can I get a copy of the test log for function testing?
tester		Are you the only person running this test?
tester		Can another person read and understand these tests?
tester		Do you update the test when you find something new?
tester		How did you receive the software for testing?
tester	1	Do you ever receive software before it is complete?
tester		How do you report a problem found to the programmer?
tester		Does the programmer review the test plan?
tester		Does the programmer get the steps used to get to the problem?
tester		Does the programmer understand your job?
tester		Does the programmer explain if you didn't test correctly?
tester		Do you ever find a difference between the design document and the module?
tester		How do you fix this when it happens?
tester		Do you know which modules don't work before testing?

1—It is OK to start testing before the program is complete as long as the tester is told which areas are not working. It saves time to start testing areas that are complete. This requires a good relationship between the tester and programmer.

21.3 INTEGRATION TESTING

Integration takes all the pieces of software and blends them together to make a system. They hope. If the team held their peer reviews, there will be fewer problems during integration testing. If all the programs, such as payroll and accounts receivable, work independently of one another, the problems could be at a minimum. Both are in the accounting department but the programs don't communicate with each other. Now add the general ledger and both programs communicate with it. It might be in a file transfer or a record within a file.

A plan for the integration is a must. If there is no plan it is a major risk. The first questions below check this. You might want to review the plan before the interviews. It might not be a formal document, but it should be written up so that it can be followed. The questions should be divided into two sections. The first will be the review of the plan, and the second is the interviews:

manager		Is there an integration test plan?
manager		Please make a copy of the integration test plan.
document		Is the document under configuration control?
document		Is a diagram overview of the programs included?
document		Is there a list of the equipment needed to perform the integration tests?
document		Are there setup instructions to perform the tests?
document		Does each test define the objectives?
document		Are the tests laid out in steps with boxes to be checked when completed?
document		Is known information (or results) used in the tests?
document		Are the results of the test shown?
document	1	Are data walls defined for checking the values?
document		Is each program drawn into the test one at a time?
document		Can any program be used first?
document		Does the test build up to all programs running as a system?

1—Data walls are used to see if information is being passed between different modules. Information is placed into a record and another module pulls the record to create a report. If the report is not correct, the testers can go back to the data wall to see if the information was stored correctly. If it is correct, the error is on the report side of the wall. If the data is wrong in the record, the problem is in the program storing the record. Hence, the name used is data wall. Which side of the wall is the problem on? Questions to ask:

tester		Do you have an integration test plan?
tester		Have you run any tests up to now?
tester		(Yes) May I see the results of the tests?
tester		Have any tests passed?
tester		Have any tests failed?
tester		(Yes) May I see a copy of the problem report?
tester		Does the report have the date and time of the test?
tester		Does the report have the name of the tester?
tester		Does the report have a good description of the problem?
tester		Does the report have the events leading up to the problem?
tester		Does the report have a status code?
tester		Who gets a copy of the problem report?
tester		Are any metrics taken during the testing?
auditor		Review the metrics.
tester		Are the metrics understandable?
tester		Do the metrics help the development process?
tester		Can the metrics be proven?
tester		Who receives the metrics?
tester		Is the test area clean and organized?
tester		Is the test system in the same configuration as the final product?
tester		What is the schedule time for completion of integration?
tester		How long has the testing taken?
tester		Will you make schedule? Completion date?

tester		How much longer will it be?
tester		Have the programmers been responsive to problems?
tester		How many problems have been found?
tester		How long does it take to get a problem resolved?
tester		How do you receive the software?
tester		Do you get it from configuration control?
tester		Do you restart the test computer each day?
tester		Do you test with different configurations?
tester		Do you test with different operating systems?
tester	1	Do you load test the software?
tester		Is the software testing started from the beginning each time new software is received?
tester		Are you using test cases?
tester		Who writes the test cases?
tester		How do you report problems with test cases?

1—This is loading the system to its fullest configuration or transactional limits.

The integration testing will probably be the longest of all the testing. Look at this process as putting a motor together for the first time. Each part is engineered to do its job and fit. The team that does the final assembly has to make adjustments to get it to work. The better the engineering team, the shorter the assembly. The system is the same way. All of the programs have to come together to create the system. In most systems, the parts will come together, but there will be adjustments. The testers need to know the product at the system level. Besides the normal testing, they need to be looking at the approved design to make sure that it was followed.

A poorly designed system will take longer in integration testing than it took development to write the code. The system will continually go back to designers to be redesigned and back to the programmers to make the changes. This becomes a patchwork quilt. Each additional fix causes more testing and retesting. If the design team does not understand the complete system with the design changes that were made after it went to programming, they could be slowing the system or causing other problems.

21.4 ACCEPTANCE TESTING

The acceptance test is run against the functional specification. This will prove that the system is ready for delivery to the customer. There should be a plan for these tests made directly from the functional specification. It should be a checklist of every function the customer requested with the features as explained. After a company gets this test running, they will ask the customer to send someone to witness the running of the test. When the customer accepts this test as completed, the software is ready for delivery. Sometimes this also means there is a milestone where the customer will make a major payment.

This test is skipped by many companies; they feel that all the other tests are good enough. Then after the software is delivered, the customer comes back and refuses to make payment until the problems are fixed. This could lead to trips back and forth to the customer's site. If there is no acceptance test, you write up the risk. Questions to ask:

tester		Do you have a copy of the functional specifications?
manager		Do you have an acceptance test document?
auditor		Get a copy and compare it to the functional specifications.
document		Does the functional specification match the test plan?
document		Is there a checklist for each function point?
document		Does the document show the setup procedure to run the test?
document		Does the document show the input data?
document		Does the document show the reports?
document		Is the entry data linked to the results shown in the reports?
document		Does the test system setup show the customer's configuration?
document	1	Is the database empty when the test starts?
document		Does the document call for the user manual?
document	2	Does the document explain the order to load the database files?
document		Does the system have a backdoor password?

document		Does the document show error input with results/messages?
tester		Is the test system in exactly the customer's configuration?
tester		Do you have information to enter to set up the database?
tester	3	Is the data supplied by the customer?
tester		Is the data on copies of customer documents?
tester	4	Are you entering the data as the system administrator or user?
tester	5	Are there different levels of operators?
tester		What are the levels?
tester		How are you testing the different levels?
tester	6	Are you testing with the same equipment that the customer will use?
tester		Is there a system log on the test system?
tester		May I see the incident reports for this testing?

1—This is the way the customer will see the system for the first time. This way you see if the programs can create everything in the database.

2—One program builds on the next and you can waste a lot of time going back to edit database records (or rows). An example would be entering the suppliers before the inventory, so the name of the supplier can be entered in the item's record.

3—The best data to work with is the customer's. This is the way the system will be used.

4—If the data is being entered with the tester logged on as an administrator, will it work for a normal user?

5—Operator levels are a security issue. Each program must be tested for the different levels.

6—Run the first report at the customer office and it might come out of the printer a mess with columns not lining up. The customer is using an old printer or one from a manufacturer different from the one the test lab used. The lab can test the reports in different operating systems with different printers.

21.5 REGRESSION TESTING

Regression testing is performed after a change or a new module is added to a system. These tests make sure that the new software has not broken any other modules. There have been guesses that 50 percent of changes in a system will break some other module.

The tests for each module should be documented so that the tests can be rerun with each addition of software. The tests become a total system test or acceptance test by the end. This part of the system testing can be a major cost if not done correctly and with a lot of planning.

When the regression test is completed, the testers know that the new module is being tested to a known system. The test also shows that the new software has not created a problem within the original modules. The tester is running the integration on the new software and not hitting incidents from the other modules. Questions to ask:

tester		Do you run regression tests?
tester		How often are they run?
tester		How do you run the tests?
tester		Do you start from the beginning each time?
tester		Are all the paths through the software tested?
tester		How are the regression test sheets maintained?
tester		Do you run all the tests each time there is a regression test?
tester		Do you keep a run log for all the regression tests?
tester		How do you log problems?
tester		How do you report the problems?
tester		Do you allow programmers to research the problem on your test system?
tester		Do you reload all the modules before you run the tests?
tester		How often do you reload the database?
tester		Do the configuration tables change during testing?

21.6 AUTOMATED TESTING

This is the hottest discussion in the software test world. If automated testing is not used at the auditee, it is not a problem.

Don't get me wrong—automated testing is a great way to do regression testing. There are many companies marketing these tools. To be able to set up a system, start the test, go home, and come back the next day to find 10 hours of testing completed can save in many ways.

There is a major commitment involved in automated testing—the cost and training will be high. The company needs to weigh that against the return on investment. I have used these tools and cut my testing time almost in half.

Automated testing is used for regression testing and exercising routines (load testing). If a module is working and you know the results, an automated test can be developed to repeat your initial test. The automated testing tool can run tables (from a spreadsheet) of different parameters to test the acceptance ranges of routines and exercise formulas. Automated testing cannot be run against a module that has never been tested before. The tool must have the result information to compare to its test results.

These questions are to be used if the company is using automated testing:

tester		Do you have automated testing?
tester		What package are you using?
tester		How long have you been using it?
tester		How many test scripts do you have now?
tester		May I see a few?
tester		Please print out a copy of the directory for scripts.
tester		How are the scripts controlled?
tester		Do you have a programmer for writing scripts?
tester		Who else writes scripts?
tester		Are the scripts reviewed by anyone?
tester		Who reviews the test scripts?
tester		How are the results saved?
tester		How often do you run the scripts?
tester		How long does it take to run the tests?
tester		Do you run them unattended?
tester		Nighttime or daytime?

tester		How do you know you have an error or problem?
tester		How do you write up problems?
tester		May I have a copy of the last three problem reports?
tester		When do you start writing a new script?
tester	1	How do you start to write a script?
tester		Do you test or have reviews for the scripts?
tester		Are you using only the record function of the tool?
tester	2	Do you run tables through the scripts?
tester		Where do you get the table data?
tester		How do you store the test data?
tester		Does the script test error entries?
tester		Do you have a parent program that controls which scripts run?
tester		Do you have a schedule or plan to run the scripts?
tester		Are all tests logged for the length of time run?
tester		Does anyone review the logs? Who? When?
tester		Do you run the same scripts for all products?
tester	3	What happens when the program is changed?
tester		Do you use the scripts to test performance? How?
tester		Does the tool help with testing the product?
tester		Are you happy with the tool?

1—Many automated test programs allow the program to record keystrokes and screens to give the writer a head start.

2—Some automated tools allow the program to use tables created by spreadsheets. This gives the testing program more flexibility to enter ranges and combinations of data.

3—When a program is changed, the test script usually must be changed. If the answer is "We never need to make changes," something is not right. Start digging for more information.

> A group of the testers (not knowing the automated tool) ran the set-up part of the test tool, which goes out to the program and reads the variables. It takes about 10 minutes to perform this the first time the programs are loaded. The testers then believed that they had tested the whole program. They did not understand the scripting part of the tool. Thank goodness they had only been using the tool two months!

The second set of questions is used if they don't have automated test tools:

test manager		Why don't you have an automated test tool?
test manager		Can this product be run with an automated test tool?
test manager		How often do you run regression tests?
test manager		Do you exercise routines when regression testing?
test manager		How many hours do you perform regression testing?
test manager		Do you read the test plan every time you run regression tests?
test manager		How do you run performance testing?

21.7 PERFORMANCE TESTING

"Software project managers will always face the reality, however, that customers are interested in price, functions, and schedule before they get the system, but after delivery they are interested in throughput, response time, and availability."[3]

Performance testing is the common sense section of testing. If there is a performance specification, the test listed should be run and results recorded. If there

---

[3]Joseph M. Juran and A. Blanton Godfrey, ed., *Juran's Quality Handbook,* 5th ed. (New York: McGraw Hill, 1999), 20.9.

is no performance specification, then common sense takes over and testers see what the system can do, matching the results of this testing against normal loads with peak times. Can the system handle the load?

Look at the original specifications and see the planned system. Find out how big a system it is expected to become. Ask how many reads, writes, and lookups are expected during an hour of normal operation. When you do a lookup, how many other files are also being queried? Take a calculator and figure out the number of times per minute the disk is being hit. Compare that number to what the design states as total hits.

There are tools to help put a load on a system to check response time. You can build a test system that can help figure out the time you need for the product. If the system calls for 100 PCs running, what happens at 150 PCs? Hopefully, all businesses will grow and more devices will be added. Will the new system handle the increase?

An example is a system that was set up for 10,000 disk reads and writes per minute. One of the first installations did 12,000 and maxed out. There were miscalculations of the number of read/writes and there was no built-in growth factor. The server was reworked and the problem was fixed with 16,000 normal read/writes able to go to 24,000 without slowing the system. If the number went higher, the system queued up the data to get over the peak in/outputs slowing the system, but not crashing it.

Even if there is no performance test plan, go through the questions for some background information. There could be some risk in this area that has not been brought to the surface:

		Is there a performance specification?
		Is there a performance plan?
		How many read, writes, and lookups per minute for this system?
		How big are the records?
		How big are the files?
		Do you monitor the CPU usage?
		What is the planned CPU usage going to be?
	1	Do you monitor the memory usage for leaks?
		Are you monitoring sensors in the system?
		How often do you poll the sensors?
		How many sensors are in the system?

		How many PCs will be connected to this system?
		What percentage of the time will the PCs be connected to the system?
		How do you know the network can carry the system?
		Is a log of system errors kept?
		Do you use scaled volume tests?
		Do you run full load tests? How?
		Does the system ever slow down for no reason?
		Do you lose data during volume tests?
		Does the PC slow down during lookups?
		Are there time gaps in the running of the software?

1—There is a monitoring tool in the control panel that the developer should use to help run performance tests.

Final Thoughts

This book was written because of my passion for quality. Auditing is the final step in securing a high-quality, profitable, and usable product.

I believe in the old sayings "haste makes waste" and a "job worth doing is worth doing well." If you are a project manager reading this book, build frequent audits into your schedule. Think of them as having the boss looking over your shoulder—but without all the negative stress that visualization can evoke. Take the time to do a thorough plan and you will be rewarded with the satisfaction of knowing you gave your project every opportunity to produce a quality product.

To the auditors and would be auditors: While this book should be used as a guide while you navigate the many types and applications of auditing, don't be limited by it. Anyone who knows me knows that I value "out of the box" thinking. Therefore, be flexible, be inventive, and be creative as you formulate the questions that will help in your work.

Index

Belong to the Quality Community!

Established in 1946, ASQ is a global community of quality experts in all fields and industries. ASQ is dedicated to the promotion and advancement of quality tools, principles, and practices in the workplace and in the community.

The Society also serves as an advocate for quality. Its members have informed and advised the U.S. Congress, government agencies, state legislatures, and other groups and individuals worldwide on quality-related topics.

Vision

By making quality a global priority, an organizational imperative, and a personal ethic, ASQ becomes the community of choice for everyone who seeks quality technology, concepts, or tools to improve themselves and their world.

ASQ is...

- More than 90,000 individuals and 700 companies in more than 100 countries

- The world's largest organization dedicated to promoting quality

- A community of professionals striving to bring quality to their work and their lives

- The administrator of the Malcolm Baldrige National Quality Award

- A supporter of quality in all sectors including manufacturing, service, healthcare, government, and education

- YOU

Visit www.asq.org for more information.

ASQ Membership

Research shows that people who join associations experience increased job satisfaction, earn more, and are generally happier*. ASQ membership can help you achieve this while providing the tools you need to be successful in your industry and to distinguish yourself from your competition. So why wouldn't you want to be a part of ASQ?

Networking

Have the opportunity to meet, communicate, and collaborate with your peers within the quality community through conferences and local ASQ section meetings, ASQ forums or divisions, ASQ Communities of Quality discussion boards, and more.

Professional Development

Access a wide variety of professional development tools such as books, training, and certifications at a discounted price. Also, ASQ certifications and the ASQ Career Center help enhance your quality knowledge and take your career to the next level.

Solutions

Find answers to all your quality problems, big and small, with ASQ's Knowledge Center, mentoring program, various e-newsletters, *Quality Progress* magazine, and industry-specific products.

Access to Information

Learn classic and current quality principles and theories in ASQ's Quality Information Center (QIC), *ASQ Weekly* e-newsletter, and product offerings.

Advocacy Programs

ASQ helps create a better community, government, and world through initiatives that include social responsibility, Washington advocacy, and Community Good Works.

Visit www.asq.org/membership for more information on ASQ membership.

*2008, The William E. Smith Institute for Association Research

ASQ Certification

ASQ certification is formal recognition by ASQ that an individual has demonstrated a proficiency within, and comprehension of, a specified body of knowledge at a point in time. Nearly 150,000 certifications have been issued. ASQ has members in more than 100 countries, in all industries, and in all cultures. ASQ certification is internationally accepted and recognized.

Benefits to the Individual

- New skills gained and proficiency upgraded
- Investment in your career
- Mark of technical excellence
- Assurance that you are current with emerging technologies
- Discriminator in the marketplace
- Certified professionals earn more than their uncertified counterparts
- Certification is endorsed by more than 125 companies

Benefits to the Organization

- Investment in the company's future
- Certified individuals can perfect and share new techniques in the workplace
- Certified staff are knowledgeable and able to assure product and service quality

Quality is a global concept. It spans borders, cultures, and languages. No matter what country your customers live in or what language they speak, they demand quality products and services. You and your organization also benefit from quality tools and practices. Acquire the knowledge to position yourself and your organization ahead of your competition.

Certifications Include

- Biomedical Auditor – CBA
- Calibration Technician – CCT
- HACCP Auditor – CHA
- Pharmaceutical GMP Professional – CPGP
- Quality Inspector – CQI
- Quality Auditor – CQA
- Quality Engineer – CQE
- Quality Improvement Associate – CQIA
- Quality Technician – CQT
- Quality Process Analyst – CQPA
- Reliability Engineer – CRE
- Six Sigma Black Belt – CSSBB
- Six Sigma Green Belt – CSSGB
- Software Quality Engineer – CSQE
- Manager of Quality/Organizational Excellence – CMQ/OE

Visit www.asq.org/certification to apply today!

ASQ Training

Classroom-based Training

ASQ offers training in a traditional classroom setting on a variety of topics. Our instructors are quality experts and lead courses that range from one day to four weeks, in several different cities. Classroom-based training is designed to improve quality and your organization's bottom line. Benefit from quality experts; from comprehensive, cutting-edge information; and from peers eager to share their experiences.

Web-based Training

Virtual Courses

ASQ's virtual courses provide the same expert instructors, course materials, interaction with other students, and ability to earn CEUs and RUs as our classroom-based training, without the hassle and expenses of travel. Learn in the comfort of your own home or workplace. All you need is a computer with Internet access and a telephone.

Self-paced Online Programs

These online programs allow you to work at your own pace while obtaining the quality knowledge you need. Access them whenever it is convenient for you, accommodating your schedule.

Some Training Topics Include

- Auditing
- Basic Quality
- Engineering
- Education
- Healthcare
- Government
- Food Safety
- ISO
- Leadership
- Lean
- Quality Management
- Reliability
- Six Sigma
- Social Responsibility

Visit www.asq.org/training for more information.